The Happy Hiccups

Napoleon Hill (born Oliver Napoleon Hill) was born in 1883 in Southwest Virginia. Most famous for authoring the self-help book *Think & Grow Rich* (1937), he was an American entrepreneur who authored other books including *The Law of Success* (1928) and *Outwitting the Devil* (1938).

The Happy Hiccups

YOUR HACK TO LIVING AN AWESOME LIFE

NAPOLEON HILL

Published by
Rupa Publications India Pvt. Ltd 2024
7/16, Ansari Road, Daryaganj
New Delhi 110002

Sales centres:
Bengaluru Chennai
Hyderabad Jaipur Kathmandu
Kolkata Mumbai Prayagraj

Edition copyright © Rupa Publications India Pvt. Ltd 2024

All rights reserved.
No part of this publication may be reproduced, transmitted,
or stored in a retrieval system, in any form or by any means,
electronic, mechanical, photocopying, recording or otherwise,
without the prior permission of the publisher.

P-ISBN: 978-93-6156-952-4

First impression 2024

10 9 8 7 6 5 4 3 2 1

Printed in India

This book is sold subject to the condition that it shall not,
by way of trade or otherwise, be lent, resold, hired out, or otherwise
circulated, without the publisher's prior consent, in any form of
binding or cover other than that in which it is published.

Contents

Part I
Laying the Bedrock for Success

1. The North Star of Achievement — 3
2. Trusting in Miracles — 28

Part II
Navigating the Road to Success

3. Rocking Your Own Boat — 43
4. Fueling Success with Passion — 73
5. Sunshine in Your Pocket — 92
6. Unleashing Collective Brilliance — 119

Part III
People Skills for Stellar Success

7. Plotting Your Course to Greatness — 137
8. Dancing in the Rain — 142

Part IV
Sustaining Lifelong Success

9. Crafting Bridges to Success — 159
10. The Symphony of Success — 165

11. Nurturing Your Greatest Asset 174
12. Footprints in the Sands of Time 187

PART I

Laying the Bedrock for Success

1

The North Star of Achievement

The power of definiteness of purpose is both awe-inspiring and transformative. It distinguishes great leaders from those who merely drift through life without direction. Leaders across all fields and eras have achieved their greatness by aligning their abilities and efforts behind a clear and specific major purpose. This purpose serves as their guiding star, steering them through challenges and setbacks.

On the other hand, those who are labeled as failures often lack such a defined purpose. They wander aimlessly, akin to a ship adrift without a rudder, returning empty-handed to their starting points repeatedly. Some may initially set out with a purpose, but they abandon it at the first sign of difficulty or opposition. They surrender without realizing that setbacks are temporary and can serve as opportunities for growth and learning.

Definiteness of purpose, coupled with the habit of going the extra mile, creates a force that defies imagination. These principles are not standalone but are part of a cohesive philosophy of success, akin to the reliability and precision found in mathematical rules. Temporary defeat, far from being the end, becomes a crucible for testing resilience and determination. The power of definiteness of purpose derives from deep psychological principles. It taps into the subconscious mind's ability to focus energy and attention towards a specific goal. When combined with other principles of achievement, such as persistence, enthusiasm, and a positive mental attitude, it forms a chain of interconnected strengths that amplify personal potential and effectiveness.

Ultimately, embracing definiteness of purpose empowers individuals to harness their inner drive and capabilities towards meaningful goals. It transforms challenges into stepping stones and setbacks into opportunities for growth. This philosophy not only shapes personal success but also serves as a blueprint for achieving extraordinary outcomes and leaving a lasting impact on the world.

Let's explore the analysis of the power of definiteness of purpose and the psychological principles underlying it, based on the premises laid out:

1. **Adoption of a Definite Purpose**: The starting point of all individual achievement is the conscious decision to adopt a clear and specific purpose, coupled with a well-defined plan for its attainment. This purpose serves as a guiding beacon, directing all efforts and actions towards a singular objective.
2. **Motives Driving Achievement**: All achievement is propelled by motives—inner drives that spur voluntary actions. These motives are fundamental and can vary, encompassing desires for wealth, recognition, self-expression, and more. Understanding and aligning these motives with one's definite purpose enhance motivation and persistence.
3. **The Power of Repetition and Emotion**: Any dominant idea or purpose held consistently in the mind, infused

with strong emotional intensity and a burning desire for realization, impresses upon the subconscious mind. This subconscious imprinting prompts automatic action and engagement towards achieving the desired outcome.

4. **Absolute Faith in Realization**: When a clear purpose is consciously held with unwavering faith in its attainment, the subconscious mind immediately takes charge. Historical evidence suggests that such resolute desires, backed by absolute faith, have consistently led to their fulfillment, underscoring the potency of belief in shaping outcomes.

5. **Control over Thought**: The power of thought is unparalleled in its influence over one's life. Individuals possess complete and unquestionable control over their thoughts, which constitutes a profound connection between the human mind and the Universal Mind of Infinite Intelligence. Faith acts as the bridge between personal thought and the greater intelligence that pervades the universe.

6. **The Subconscious Mind as a Gateway**: The subconscious mind serves as the conduit to Infinite Intelligence. It operates in direct response to one's faith and instructions, akin to interacting with a separate entity within oneself. This aspect highlights the profound influence of faith in accessing and directing subconscious processes towards achieving goals.

7. **Wisdom in Action**: A definite purpose, fortified by absolute faith, embodies wisdom in action. This wisdom manifests in deliberate, focused efforts that yield positive outcomes. It underscores the principle that purposeful action guided by faith aligns with the natural laws of success and achievement.

These premises elucidate the profound impact of definiteness of purpose coupled with unwavering faith. They underscore the role of motive, emotion, repetition, and belief in harnessing the power of the subconscious mind and aligning personal aspirations with universal forces. This framework not only guides individual achievement but also underscores the interconnectedness between human potential and the infinite possibilities of the universe.

The clear benefits of definiteness of purpose are manifold:

1. **Development of Essential Qualities**: Definiteness of purpose cultivates self-reliance, personal initiative, imagination, enthusiasm, self-discipline, and concentrated effort—essential attributes for achieving material success.
2. **Effective Time Management**: It encourages meticulous time management and daily planning aimed at advancing one's major life purpose.
3. **Enhanced Opportunity Recognition**: It sharpens awareness of opportunities aligned with one's major purpose, instilling the courage to seize them when they arise.
4. **Facilitation of Cooperation**: It fosters cooperation from others, as a clear purpose attracts support and collaboration.
5. **Promotion of Faith**: By fostering a positive mindset and eliminating fear, doubt, and indecision, definiteness of purpose paves the way for the development of faith—a critical component in achieving goals.
6. **Cultivation of Success Consciousness**: It instills a consciousness of success, essential for sustained achievement in any endeavor.
7. **Elimination of Procrastination**: Definiteness of purpose eradicates the detrimental habit of procrastination, ensuring proactive pursuit of goals.
8. **Nurturing a Positive Mental Attitude**: Above all, it directly contributes to the cultivation and continual maintenance

of a positive mental attitude—the cornerstone of enduring success and fulfillment.

Definiteness of purpose encompasses a host of critical attributes, pivotal to achieving success in various facets of life. While its primary traits include self-reliance, initiative, imagination, enthusiasm, self-discipline, and focused effort, its significance extends far beyond these foundational qualities.

Sound physical health, harmony in relationships, freedom from fear, hope of future achievement, capacity for faith, willingness to share blessings, labor of love as occupation, open-mindedness, self-discipline, capacity to understand others, and sufficient financial resources—all these treasures are within reach when guided by a clear and unwavering purpose.

Reflecting on the notable achievers throughout history, particularly those from this country, reveals a common thread: a relentless focus on a major purpose. From industrialists to inventors, leaders to artists, their dedication to a singular objective propelled them forward. Their stories underscore the transformative power of definiteness of purpose in shaping destinies and leaving lasting legacies.

HOW TO ACQUIRE A DEFINITE MAJOR PURPOSE

Acquiring a Definite Major Purpose is a deliberate process that requires commitment and clarity. Here's a detailed guide to help you embark on this transformative journey.

Write Out Your Major Purpose

Begin by writing a complete, clear, and definitive statement of your **MAJOR PURPOSE IN LIFE**. This statement should encapsulate your deepest aspirations and ambitions. Sign it as a commitment to yourself and commit it to memory. Repeat it daily, reinforcing your belief in its realization through your connection with Infinite Intelligence. Repetition solidifies your faith and aligns your thoughts with your purpose.

Develop a Clear Plan

Draft a precise and actionable plan outlining how you intend to achieve your Major Purpose. Specify the timeframe within which you aim to accomplish it. Include detailed steps and milestones that mark your journey towards fulfillment. Equally important, articulate what you are willing to give in return for achieving your purpose. Recognize that every goal demands an investment, whether it's time, effort, resources, or sacrifices.

Maintain Flexibility in Your Approach

While your plan provides a structured path forward, remain open to inspiration and opportunities for improvement. Understand that Infinite Intelligence may present you with unforeseen insights or opportunities. Be ready to adapt and embrace superior plans that align more closely with your ultimate objective. Flexibility ensures you can capitalize on unexpected developments and refine your strategies for greater effectiveness.

Maintain Confidentiality

Keep your Major Purpose and detailed plans private, sharing them only with individuals involved in your journey or those who can provide valuable guidance and support. However, be prepared to leverage the Master Mind Principle, which involves collaborating with like-minded individuals to amplify your efforts and receive constructive feedback.

By following these steps diligently, you empower yourself to articulate, pursue, and achieve a Definite Major Purpose that not only directs your actions but also enriches your life with purpose and fulfillment. Each day's commitment strengthens your resolve and brings you closer to manifesting your dreams into reality.

MASTER MIND PRINCIPLE

It is essential not to dismiss these instructions simply because they may seem unfamiliar. Follow them meticulously, in earnest, knowing you are mirroring the practices of many of this nation's greatest leaders.

These instructions require no effort beyond your capability. They do not demand more time or ability than the average person can provide. Moreover, they are fully aligned with the principles espoused by all genuine religions.

Begin by defining precisely what you desire from life and what you are prepared to offer in return. Determine your destination and chart your course to get there. Take your first steps from where you currently stand, utilizing whatever resources are readily available to you. As you apply these resources, you will find that additional and superior means will progressively reveal themselves.

This has been the pathway of every individual recognized globally as a success. Many of them embarked from humble beginnings, armed primarily with an impassioned aspiration to achieve a specific objective. Such a desire holds enduring power.

Finally, bear in mind:

'The Moving Finger writes; and, having writ,
Moves on: nor all thy Piety nor Wit
Shall lure it back to cancel half a Line,
Nor all thy Tears wash out a Word of it.'

These words underscore the irrevocable nature of time and the importance of decisive action in shaping your destiny. Embrace the Master Mind Principle with conviction, and you will unlock its transformative potential in your journey towards success and fulfillment.

Yesterday has gone forever! Tomorrow will never arrive, but Today is yesterday's Tomorrow within your reach. What are you doing with it?

Presently, I shall reveal to you a principle which is the keystone to the arch of all great achievements; the principle which has been responsible for our great American way of life; our system of free enterprise; our riches and our freedom. But first, let us ensure that you are clear about what you desire from life.

Ideas that Lead to Success Begin as Definiteness of Purpose

It is a well-known fact that ideas are the only assets which have no fixed values. They are the beginning of all achievements, the foundation of fortunes, and the genesis of inventions. Ideas have transcended the air above us and the oceans around us; they have empowered us to harness the ether, enabling brain-to-brain communication through telepathy.

ALL IDEAS BEGIN AS THE RESULT OF DEFINITENESS OF PURPOSE

When you have a clear, definite purpose, ideas crystallize. They take shape and form, driven by your unwavering commitment to your goal. It is this clarity of purpose that sets the stage for creativity, innovation, and breakthroughs. Every great achievement, from the grandest inventions to the most profound societal advancements, traces its origins to someone's clear and resolute purpose.

Consider the Wright brothers, driven by their unwavering purpose to achieve powered flight. It was their singular focus that led them to conceive, design, and eventually realize the dream of flight, forever altering human transportation.

Similarly, look at the pioneers of technology who envisioned a world connected through the internet. Their definiteness of purpose propelled them to create the frameworks and protocols that now underpin global communication.

In your own journey, clarity of purpose will be your guiding star. It will align your thoughts, actions, and decisions toward a singular aim, giving you the resilience and determination needed to overcome obstacles and seize opportunities.

Therefore, embrace Definiteness of Purpose as the foundation of your aspirations. Cultivate it with unwavering dedication, and watch as your ideas transform into reality, shaping a future that aligns with your deepest desires and ambitions.

The talking machine remained merely an abstract idea until Edison, driven by definiteness of purpose, organized it and submitted it to his subconscious mind. Through this process, it tapped into the vast reservoir of Infinite Intelligence, from which a practical plan was revealed to him. With meticulous attention, he translated this plan into a functional machine that revolutionized communication.

Similarly, the philosophy of individual achievement originated as a seed in Andrew Carnegie's mind. His unwavering definiteness of purpose propelled this idea forward, transforming it into a guiding principle that now benefits millions worldwide. This philosophy not only empowers individuals but also stands poised to become a transformative force on a global scale, guiding countless amidst turbulent times marked by uncertainty and potential defeatism.

Consider the discovery of the North American continent, once a distant dream conceived by a humble sailor. Backed by his definitive purpose, this idea manifested into reality, bringing vast lands under the influence of civilization. Today, this historical idea continues to hold promise, potentially elevating our nation to a pivotal role as civilization's last frontier and a beacon of human liberty worldwide.

Indeed, every idea held in the mind, whether feared, revered, or emphasized, begins to take shape in the physical realm. This fundamental truth applies universally, from personal aspirations to national destinies. It underscores the importance for those striving to overcome poverty and adversity to maintain focus on positive beliefs and aspirations. For what people believe, discuss, and fear possesses the power to manifest itself, shaping destinies both individually and collectively.

SELF-SUGGESTION: BRIDGING THE CONSCIOUS AND SUBCONSCIOUS MIND

The talking machine remained merely an abstract idea until Edison, driven by definiteness of purpose, organized it and submitted it to his subconscious mind. Through this process, it tapped into the vast reservoir of Infinite Intelligence, from which a practical plan was revealed to him. With meticulous attention, he translated this plan into a functional machine that revolutionized communication.

Similarly, the philosophy of individual achievement originated as a seed in Andrew Carnegie's mind. His unwavering definiteness of purpose propelled this idea forward, transforming it into a guiding principle that now benefits millions worldwide. This philosophy not only empowers individuals but also stands poised to become a transformative force on a global scale, guiding countless amidst turbulent times marked by uncertainty and potential defeatism.

Consider the discovery of the North American continent, once a distant dream conceived by a humble sailor. Backed by his definitive purpose, this idea manifested into reality, bringing vast lands under the influence of civilization. Today, this historical idea continues to hold promise, potentially elevating our nation to a pivotal role as civilization's last frontier and a beacon of human liberty worldwide.

Indeed, every idea held in the mind, whether feared, revered, or emphasized, begins to take shape in the physical realm. This fundamental truth applies universally, from personal aspirations to national destinies. It underscores the importance for those striving to overcome poverty and adversity to maintain focus on positive beliefs and aspirations. For what people believe, discuss, and fear possesses the power to manifest itself, shaping destinies both individually and collectively.

Psychologists and scientists firmly reject the notion of miracles, steadfast in their belief that every event, no matter how extraordinary, stems from a discernible cause, albeit one that may not yet be fully understood. Despite this stance, it remains widely accepted that individuals who cultivate a mindset of faith, thereby liberating themselves from self-imposed limitations, often discover solutions to their problems, irrespective of their complexity.

Furthermore, psychologists emphasize that Infinite Intelligence, while not characterized as a solver of riddles, reliably carries out any well-defined idea, aim, purpose, or desire entrusted to the subconscious mind with unwavering faith. This understanding underscores the profound impact of having a clear, definite purpose combined with steadfast belief in its attainment.

It is important to grasp that Infinite Intelligence operates strictly according to the instructions it receives from the conscious mind. It does not alter or modify thoughts but responds faithfully to ideas and desires that are clearly defined and backed by unshakable faith. This realization empowers individuals to confront and resolve their challenges with greater ease than those who are mired in worry and uncertainty.

'Hunches,' often regarded as intuitive nudges, are signals that Infinite Intelligence is attempting to communicate with the conscious mind. These intuitive prompts typically arise in response to thoughts, plans, desires, or fears that have been deeply ingrained in the subconscious. They serve as subtle reminders or insights, conveying valuable information that may have originated from a previously submitted thought or intention.

All hunches should be treated with respect and carefully examined, as they often carry significant insights or solutions that can benefit the individual. Interestingly, these intuitive insights may manifest hours, days, or even weeks after the initial thought was submitted to Infinite Intelligence, a testament to its intricate workings and responsiveness.

This subject invites contemplation and meditation, gradually revealing its depth to those who engage with it thoughtfully and persistently. Understanding these dynamics opens doors to harnessing the power of Infinite Intelligence for personal growth and problem-solving.

Understanding the principle of mental operation described here provides a reliable insight into why meditation sometimes manifests desired outcomes, while at other times, it seems to attract undesired results. This profound understanding of the mind's workings is achieved through disciplined preparation, a process detailed in a formula I will discuss later.

A fundamental truth of the world is that the circumstances of both individuals and collective society conform to the precise patterns of their thoughts. Successful individuals achieve their goals because they cultivate a habit of thinking in terms of success. Definiteness of purpose plays a crucial role here—it should occupy the mind so completely that there is no room for thoughts of failure.

Moreover, another profound truth emerges: even those who have faced defeat and see themselves as failures can transform adversity into a force that propels them toward success. By metaphorically adjusting the 'sails' of their minds, they harness the winds of challenge and convert them into a powerful momentum forward. As the saying goes,

> 'One ship sails east, the other west, Impelled by the same winds that blow, It's the set of the sails, and not the gales, That determines the way they go.'

This analogy underscores the transformative power of mindset—the ability to navigate life's challenges not by altering external circumstances, but by mastering one's internal responses and outlook.

To those who pride themselves on being 'coolheaded, practical business men,' the analysis of the principle of Definiteness of Purpose might initially seem abstract or impractical. However, underlying this principle is a power greater than conscious thought, often imperceptible to the finite mind. Embracing this truth is crucial for successfully achieving any definite purpose rooted in aspirations for great accomplishments.

Throughout history, from ancient philosophers like Plato and Socrates to modern thinkers like Emerson, and from revered statesmen such as George Washington to Abraham Lincoln, there has been a recognition of turning inward during times of great challenge. This inner reflection taps into spiritual powers inherent in the Infinite, accessed through one's 'inner self.'

We make no apologies for asserting that enduring success, whether achieved in the past or in the future, hinges upon individuals who recognize and harness these spiritual energies. Every circumstance in a person's life, whether leading to failure or success, is traceable to specific causes. Crucially, many of these causes are within an individual's control or influence.

This fundamental truth underscores the paramount importance of Definiteness of Purpose. If a person's life circumstances do not align with their desires, they possess the power to effect change by adjusting their mental attitude and cultivating new, more empowering thought patterns. This proactive approach not only reshapes individual destinies but also aligns them with the spiritual forces that guide and empower transformative achievements.

THE PATH TO SUCCESS THROUGH DEFINITENESS OF PURPOSE

Implementing the principle of Going The Extra Mile—an ideology I deeply endorse—enabled me to persuade the author to entrust me with a significant aspect of my Definite Major Purpose: spreading this transformative philosophy during a critical period of societal need.

I expressed to the author, and now to you, my profound belief that I would value authoring this philosophy over holding the office of President of the United States. Following that, I consider it a greater privilege to assist in disseminating it than to possess all the world's wealth. This privilege has been graciously bestowed upon me.

I intend to fulfill this privilege through various avenues. Firstly, I will distill the philosophy into succinct radio programs aimed at reaching a wide audience.

Furthermore, I will contribute to making the philosophy accessible through printed lessons distributed via newsstands and bookstores nationwide. Additionally, I aim to collaborate in producing educational films that convey the philosophy to industrial workers, facilitated through the cooperation of American industry management.

Moreover, I plan to support the establishment of nationwide private study clubs where the philosophy will be taught through educational films and printed materials.

Lastly, I am committed to collaborating with churches across the nation to ensure their members have access to this philosophy.

By leveraging these channels, I aim to fulfill my mission of making this philosophy widely accessible, believing in its potential to positively impact countless lives and guide individuals towards lasting success.

I have also arranged with the author of this profound philosophy to create a book tailored for children, presenting its principles in a manner that captures their imagination. This book will be widely distributed through bookstores and adapted into educational films for use in public schools across the nation.

Looking ahead, I aspire to explore further opportunities that will allow this philosophy to reach an even broader audience, ensuring it becomes accessible to every individual seeking their path in life.

Thus, I am privileged to unveil the inner workings of a mind driven by a Definite Major Purpose. While the task ahead may appear daunting, I undertake it with deep affection, viewing it as a labor of love. My reward lies not in material gain but in the ever-expanding wealth that comes from enriching the lives of others—a truth known only to those who have experienced the joy of sharing their blessings.

True wealth—the wealth of life—grows in direct proportion to the extent it benefits others. This I have witnessed firsthand; every act of giving has returned to me tenfold, enriching my life beyond measure.

In my endeavors, I seek no acclaim or recognition, preferring to serve anonymously whenever possible. My goal is not to elevate my name but to enrich my soul through meaningful service to humanity. The riches I share freely only add to the abundance of my own happiness in this blessed journey of life.

I have no desire for monuments erected in my honor once I am no longer here. Instead, I prefer to build my own monuments while I am alive—in the hearts of my fellow human beings. These monuments are not intended to glorify my name but to celebrate the spirit of Fellowship that I strive to foster for the betterment of humanity.

In this same spirit, I have established the expansive estate of Happy Valley, and I am committed to its upkeep for as long as I live. This estate stands as a testament to my belief in the power of community and fellowship.

I encourage those of you who are also seeking the path to Happy Valley to embrace this spirit of fellowship. You will discover this path most swiftly by assisting others in finding it themselves.

One of the most profound truths I have learned is that the most effective way to solve one's personal challenges is to help someone facing even greater difficulties. This principle, rooted in the habit of Going The Extra Mile, may seem simple but it possesses a captivating magic—it never fails to yield results. Yet, understanding this principle cannot be achieved through mere acceptance of my words. It requires personal adoption and application in your own life. Once you do so, you will no longer require external validation of its efficacy. You will find numerous opportunities around you. The aftermath of World War II left millions bewildered and disheartened, searching desperately for a path to happiness. Often, all it takes is a small act of kindness to reignite their hope and courage. You have the power to ignite that spark in those closest to you.

By aiding others in discovering their path, you inevitably find it for yourself. Perhaps you could initiate a Fellowship Club among your neighbors or coworkers, taking on the role of leader and mentor within the group. This simple step can have profound ripple effects in your community and beyond.

Here you will discover another profound truth: the most effective way to internalize the principles of the philosophy of individual achievement is by teaching it to others. When you take on the role of a teacher, you deepen your own understanding and mastery of the subject matter.

As a current student of this philosophy, you have the potential to evolve into a true master by imparting your knowledge to others. In doing so, you secure your own rewards in advance.

If you are employed in industry, seize this significant opportunity to find fulfillment by assisting others in cultivating peaceful and harmonious relationships. This approach is not only sound but has been consistently validated by the experiences of individuals from all walks of life. Labor sectors do not require agitators; what they truly need are peacemakers. Furthermore, they require a robust philosophy to guide their members—a philosophy that promotes mutual benefit for both management and workers alike. The principles of this philosophy are precisely tailored to serve this purpose effectively.

The labor leader who adopts and implements this philosophy to guide their followers will undoubtedly earn their trust and garner the full cooperation of their employers. Isn't this outcome self-evident? Isn't the promise of such rewards sufficient justification for adopting this philosophy?

A labor organization governed by the principles of this philosophy would bring numerous benefits to all parties involved. Discord and friction would give way to harmony in human relationships, fostering a work environment where mutual respect and understanding prevail. Agitators and those who exploit labor would naturally fade away, replaced by a culture of collaboration and shared prosperity. The organization's resources could be redirected from divisive political activities towards educating its members and fostering skill development. Imagine the potential when funds intended for defense against disruptive actions are instead invested in enhancing workers' capabilities and ensuring their well-being.

Moreover, the adoption of this philosophy would lead to more profits available for distributing as wages—profits that management would prefer to allocate to their workers as part of a fair and equitable compensation package. This shift not only enhances the financial stability of workers but also strengthens their loyalty and commitment to the organization's goals.

There is an urgent need for a Fellowship Club in every industry. In fact, many large industries could host multiple such clubs, serving as forums where workers and management come together on common ground. Membership in these clubs would foster deeper understanding and cooperation, translating directly to improved productivity and satisfaction in the workplace.

I have emphasized this specific field of opportunity because I understand that the discord between industry management and workers stands as the foremost economic challenge in our nation today. If you haven't yet embraced a Definite Major Purpose in your life, now presents an ideal opportunity to do so. Begin right where you are by sharing and teaching this philosophy to those who are in dire need of its principles. We've reached a critical juncture where it's not merely advantageous but imperative for each individual to assist their neighbor in resolving personal challenges. This collective effort is crucial for our own self-preservation and the well-being of our communities.

Consider this scenario: If your neighbor's house were engulfed in flames, you'd naturally volunteer to help extinguish the fire, regardless of your relationship with them. Common sense dictates that by saving their house, you're also safeguarding your own.

My advocacy for harmony between industry management and workers isn't solely about the interests of management. I recognize that without such harmony, the very structures of management and the roles of workers as we know them today could cease to exist in the near future.

Conversely, individuals who adopt a solid life philosophy will find themselves surrounded by an array of opportunities that were unimaginable just a decade ago. This philosophy not only fosters personal growth but also facilitates a broader societal harmony that benefits everyone involved.

The individual who ventures forth without a Definite Major Purpose will inevitably encounter challenges far greater than those faced by the average person.

In the present and future world, the most promising opportunities will undoubtedly be seized by those who adequately prepare themselves to lead in their chosen fields. Leadership in any domain requires a solid philosophical foundation. The era of random and inconsistent leadership is gone forever; instead, the evolving world demands skills, techniques, and deep human understanding.

Within the sphere of industry, foremen and supervisors must embrace new roles and responsibilities. They must not only excel in the technical aspects essential for efficient production but also in cultivating harmony among the workers they oversee.

Today's youth are the future leaders of society. What proactive measures are we taking to ensure their development? This is a profound challenge, and a significant part of addressing it rests on the shoulders of educators in public schools.

These are undeniable truths that underscore the fact that the future holds unprecedented opportunities for meaningful contributions. These opportunities arise from the imperatives of a rapidly changing world, where some may fail to grasp the full magnitude and implications of the transformations underway.

Take stock, you who have yet to define your life's purpose, and assess where you stand in this rapidly evolving world. Equip yourself for the new opportunities unfolding before you and seize them with all your might. If given the chance, I could certainly select a clear and fitting Major Purpose tailored to your skills and needs, and lay out a straightforward plan for achieving it. However, my true service to you lies in teaching you how to undertake this process independently.

In the pursuit of your purpose, the idea you seek will eventually manifest itself. This has been the experience of countless students of this philosophy. When this idea arrives, it will captivate you with such intensity that you cannot ignore it. This assurance holds true, provided your search is sincere.

One remarkable aspect of this philosophy is its ability to spark the birth of new ideas, uncover overlooked opportunities for personal advancement, and instill the drive to take initiative in seizing and maximizing those opportunities. This isn't mere chance; it's a deliberate design of the philosophy. It's clear that opportunities and ideas generated through one's own thought and effort hold greater value than those borrowed from others. The very act of creating useful ideas leads a person to discover additional sources of inspiration when needed. While having access to sources of inspiration is immensely beneficial and self-reliance is invaluable, there may come a time when one must tap into the resources of other minds. This necessity often arises for those aspiring to leadership and higher levels of personal achievement.

Let me now reveal to you the method by which personal power can be attained through harnessing the collective minds focused on specific objectives.

This very approach enabled Andrew Carnegie to usher in the era of steel and elevate it to become America's foremost industry, despite starting with no initial capital and having minimal education. Similarly, Thomas A. Edison, lacking personal expertise in fields such as physics, mathematics, chemistry, and electronics—essential for his work as an inventor—became history's most prolific inventor through this method.

Take heart in knowing that lack of formal education, financial resources, or technical proficiency need not discourage you from pursuing any major life goal. This philosophy offers a pathway through which any reasonable objective can be achieved by an individual of average ability.

However, it cannot choose your goal for you. Once you have established your own purpose, this philosophy can unquestionably guide you toward its realization—a promise without exceptions.

We cannot dictate your aspirations or specify the level of success you should seek, but we can and will impart the formula through which achievements can be attained.

Your primary responsibility at this moment is to ascertain what you truly desire in life, determine your destination, and plan your course of action upon arrival. This is a responsibility that only you can shoulder, yet it is one that ninety-eight out of every hundred people fail to undertake. This fundamental reason explains why only two percent of individuals can be deemed successful.

The foundation of success lies in Definiteness of Purpose!

The emphasis placed on this fact may seem excessive, but it stems from the pervasive tendency for ninety-eight percent of people to procrastinate and drift through life without ever defining a clear Major Purpose.

Having a single-minded focus is an invaluable asset—so valuable because so few individuals possess it. Yet, it is an asset that anyone can acquire in an instant.

Decide what you want from life, commit to achieving it without settling for substitutes, and you will have acquired one of the most priceless assets available to humanity.

However, your desire must transcend mere wishful thinking or passive hope. It must be a burning, obsessive desire—one that compels you to be willing to pay whatever price is necessary for its attainment. The cost may be significant or modest, but you must condition your mind to be prepared to pay it, no matter what it may be.

The moment you commit to your Definite Major Purpose in life, you will notice a remarkable phenomenon: pathways and strategies to achieve that purpose will begin to unfold before you.

Unexpected opportunities will present themselves. The support and cooperation of others will become readily available, and friends will appear seemingly by magic. Your fears and doubts will gradually dissipate, replaced by a sense of self-reliance and confidence.

To those unfamiliar with this process, such outcomes may seem fantastical. However, to those who have decisively chosen and pursued a clear life goal, this is not merely a promise based on observation but a reality borne out of personal experience. I speak from my own journey of transforming from a profound failure to a resounding success. Therefore, I confidently assure you that similar transformations await you if you diligently follow the roadmap provided by this philosophy.

When you reach that pivotal moment of choosing your Definite Major Purpose, do not be disheartened if close relatives or friends dismissively label you a 'dreamer.' Remember, throughout history, dreamers have consistently been the trailblazers of human progress. They have bestowed upon us the foundation of the American system of free enterprise, secured our cherished personal liberties, and endowed us with the world's most formidable air force and navy. They have expanded the boundaries of civilization and shaped the American way of life into a model that inspires envy worldwide.

Consider Christopher Columbus, who dreamed of discovering an unknown world and ventured into uncharted waters to realize his vision. Reflect on Copernicus, who envisioned an unseen cosmos and, aided by a makeshift telescope, shattered millennia-old fears and superstitions. Contemplate Thomas A. Edison, whose dream of an electrically illuminated lamp led him through ten thousand failures to finally illuminate the world.

Let no one dissuade you from dreaming, but ensure your

dreams are fortified with decisive action grounded in Definiteness of Purpose. Your prospects for success are as promising as those who came before you, if not greater. Today, you have access to the accumulated wisdom of countless achievers who painstakingly forged their paths to success.

Wise individuals are generous with their wealth, circumspect with their confidences, and judicious in their speech. They listen attentively, recognizing that valuable insights often emerge in moments of attentive silence. They understand that excessive talk seldom contributes to learning, save for illuminating the pitfalls of verbosity.

There exists a time for speaking and a time for silence, and wise individuals, when unsure, lean towards silence to give themselves the advantage.

The exchange of ideas through conversation is crucial for gathering knowledge, formulating plans towards achieving a Definite Major Purpose, and finding practical ways to execute those plans. Among achievers in the upper echelons, discussions around the 'round table' stand out as exemplary forums for such exchanges. These differ vastly from aimless conversations where individuals open their minds indiscriminately to anyone willing to engage.

Now, I will introduce you to a reliable method for exchanging thoughts with others, ensuring you receive as much as you contribute, if not more. Through this approach, not only can you freely discuss your most cherished plans, but doing so will prove beneficial for your progress.

Allow me to guide you to a crucial juncture where you can veer off the side path leading to Happy Valley and merge onto the main thoroughfare. This intersection I speak of is clearly signposted, ensuring you won't miss it.

This pivotal intersection marks the point where high

achievers diverge from many of their former associates and confidants. Instead, they align themselves with individuals who are capable of providing support and guidance on their journey towards Happy Valley.

2

Trusting in Miracles

If you had a definite major purpose, knew exactly what you wanted to do, had a mastermind alliance of people that could help you achieve it, and then possessed the sufficient faith to keep you motivated while you pursued it, that would be about all you would need. However, why do you suppose we need the fourteen additional principles? We need these fourteen additional principles to induce you to make use of these three primary ones.

You need personal initiative. You need imagination. You need enthusiasm. In other words, this philosophy is similar to baking a cake. When you bake a cake, you don't put in just one ingredient. You add a pinch of this, a pinch of that, a dash of another thing, and then you put it in the stove and bake it. If you removed any one of those ingredients, you wouldn't end up with the same kind of cake. It's the same way with this philosophy. You can't leave out any one of these seventeen principles. It would be like taking a link out of a chain. You wouldn't have a chain anymore; you'd have two parts of a chain, but not a whole chain. The other fourteen principles are supporting principles of these three.

Faith is a state of mind that has been called the mainspring of the soul, through which one's aims, desires, plans, and purposes may be translated into their physical or financial equivalent. There are the fundamentals of faith, but by applied faith, I'm referring to something vastly different from mere belief. The word applied means what? Action. It's the action part of faith. Without action, faith is nothing but just daydreaming. There are many people who believe in things but don't do anything about them, engaging only in daydreaming. Applied faith is an active faith.

FAITH AND THE FIRST THREE PRINCIPLES OF SUCCESS

1. **Definiteness of Purpose**: Purpose is supported by personal initiative and action, action, action—the more action, the better. This means continual action, not only on your part but also on the part of those who may be cooperating with you or your mastermind allies. When you have a clear and definite purpose, it serves as a guide, ensuring that every step you take is aligned with your ultimate goal.
2. **Positive Mental Attitude**: A positive mind, free from all negatives such as fear, envy, hatred, jealousy, and greed, is essential. Mental attitude determines the effectiveness of faith. It's a fact. The frame of mind that you are in when you pray will determine what happens as a result of that prayer. There's no two ways about it. You can test it for yourself and find out. I have no doubt that you have had experiences similar to mine, sending out prayers that didn't produce anything but a negative result. Do you suppose there is anybody who hasn't had that experience at one time or another? When you pray, unless you have such absolute faith

that whatever you are going after you're going to acquire, and that you can see it in advance in your possession before you start asking for it, chances are the effect of your prayer is going to be negative.

3. **Mastermind Alliance**: A mastermind alliance convenes one or more other people who radiate courage based on faith and are suited mentally and spiritually to one's needs in carrying out a given purpose. The collective energy, ideas, and support from a mastermind alliance significantly increase your chances of success. When you bring together a group of like-minded individuals who share a common purpose and possess faith in the endeavor, you create a powerful force that can overcome obstacles and achieve remarkable results.

By integrating these principles with faith, you create a robust foundation for success. Faith, when combined with definiteness of purpose, positive mental attitude, and the support of a mastermind alliance, transforms aspirations into reality. These principles act as catalysts, driving you towards your goals with unwavering confidence and relentless action.

ELEMENTS OF APPLIED FAITH

Every Adversity Carries with It the Seed of an Equivalent Benefit

Temporary defeat is not failure until it has been accepted as such. Do you know where the majority of people fall down in connection with their application of their faith? It's when they're defeated, and they accept that defeat as something they can't do anything about. Instead of beginning immediately to search for that seed of an equivalent benefit that's in every defeat, they become moody, broody, discouraged, and build up inferiority complexes. Instead, they could reverse the order and use defeat as nothing more than a temporary point from which to make another effort.

My saying that every adversity carries with it the seed of an equivalent benefit, that every defeat and every failure carries the seed of an equivalent benefit, wouldn't mean anything to you unless I made application of it and gave you illustration after illustration. If you examine enough illustrations in your own experience, you'll see that it always works out that way. That's why I want you to look closely at the adversities that come to you.

Do you know that your adversities are often your greatest blessings? Do you know the greatest blessing that ever came into my life? Of course, it was the loss of my mother. Ordinarily, the greatest catastrophe that could overtake a child would be to lose his mother at the age of nine years. However, this tragedy brought with it the seed of an equivalent benefit that became apparent over time. It instilled in me a resilience and strength that I might not have developed otherwise.

By learning to see adversities as opportunities for growth and to search for the seed of an equivalent benefit, you can transform challenges into stepping stones toward success. This perspective not only fosters resilience but also empowers you to turn setbacks into powerful motivators for achieving your goals. Embracing this principle of applied faith helps you to maintain a positive outlook and persistent effort, even in the face of difficulties, ultimately leading to greater achievements and personal growth.

Why do I say that was the greatest, greatest blessing? Because it brought me a new mother to take her place, one who is responsible for everything that I've achieved and everything that I shall achieve. Without her influence, I'd still be fighting rattlesnakes, drinking mountain liquor, and feuding. My relatives are still doing that same thing, so there's no reason to expect that I wouldn't be. I've had a lot of other adversities, and I want to tell you that without some twenty major adversities I've gone through, I would never have been able to pursue the soundness of this philosophy—that there is a seed of equivalent benefit in every adversity.

Can you imagine any worse adversity to a man than to be informed that his son was born without any signs of ears and would be a deaf and dumb mute all of his life? Can you imagine anything worse than that? I'll always be thankful that because of my contact with Infinite Intelligence, my deaf son was provided with a sort of hearing system that gave him 65 percent of his normal hearing and eventually 100 percent with a modern hearing aid. He learned to live a normal life and I got the greatest demonstration of my entire experience in the power of faith. I couldn't have gotten it any other way. I couldn't have gotten it secondhand; I had to get it firsthand.

I never accepted that affliction of that child, not even before I saw him, and not even after I saw him. I never accepted it. His relatives accepted it. They wanted to put him in the school for underprivileged children where he'd learn sign language and lip reading. I didn't even want him to know there were such things. When he was old enough to go to school, I had a fight with the school authorities every year just as regular as a clock, because they wanted to send him to a school for underprivileged children, to mix with the other children and see their afflictions. I didn't want him to know there were such things. I taught him from the very beginning that his not having any ears was a great blessing—and he believed it.

Compassion led people to do things for him they wouldn't have done otherwise. He got a job as a salesman for the Saturday Evening Post and he led every salesman throughout the United States. He'd often go out with five dollars' worth of merchandise and come back with ten dollars in cash. He did that many times. People would look at him and say, 'Why, that poor little fellow with no ears is out selling papers. I guess his parents are poor.' They'd give him a dollar bill and when he'd try to give them their change, they'd say, 'Oh, sonny, you just keep that.' So he'd often get a dollar apiece for the Saturday Evening Post. Not at all conscious today of any affliction, he's living a perfectly normal life because I taught him that an affliction, any kind of affliction, can be transmuted into a benefit.

Through this experience, I have learned firsthand that adversities can indeed be blessings in disguise. My son's journey reinforced the power of applied faith. It taught me that an unwavering belief in positive outcomes, even in the face of seemingly insurmountable challenges, can transform any situation. By instilling in my son the belief that his condition was a unique blessing, I empowered him to see opportunities where others might only see limitations. This mindset not only helped him succeed but also demonstrated to me, and hopefully to you, the incredible potential of faith when applied with determination and a positive attitude.

Affirmation of Definite Major Purpose

Applied faith requires the habit of affirming one's definite major purpose in the form of a prayer at least once daily. The subconscious mind only knows what you tell it, or what you allow other people to tell it, or what you allow the circumstances of life to tell it. It doesn't know the difference between a lie and the truth. It doesn't know the difference between a penny and a million dollars. It accepts the things that you send over, and if you send over predominating thoughts on poverty, ill health, and failure, that's exactly what you'll get. No matter how much faith you may have later on, you'll find out the subconscious responds to the mental attitude that you're maintaining during the day. It's necessary for you to affirm over and over again the objects that you are going to attain in life until you educate your subconscious mind to automatically attract to you the things that are related to what you're aiming to attain in life. You'll find that your mind is like an electrode magnet and once you charge it with a clear picture of what you want, it'll attract to you from the highways and the byways the things that you need to carry out that purpose.

Recognition of Infinite Intelligence

Recognition of the existence of an Infinite Intelligence that gives order to the vast, entire universe. You are a minute expression of this intelligence and as such your mind has no limitation except those accepted or set up in your own mind. Let me repeat that statement: your mind has no limitations whatsoever, except those that you allow to be established there or that you deliberately set up in your mind or accept. That's a pretty broad statement. However, the achievements of men like Mr. Edison, Mr. Ford, Mr. Carnegie, and Napoleon Hill (if you please) definitely support the idea that there is no limitation except that which you set up in your mind.

If I had ever wavered for one second in my belief of what I would do, from the time that I started with Mr. Carnegie up until the time I gave this philosophy to the world, I would never have done it. How did I do it? Do you have any idea what played the strongest part in what I've achieved? It wasn't my brilliance and it wasn't my outstanding intelligence. I have no more brilliance than the average person and no more intelligence than the average person. But I believed that I could do it and I never stopped believing it. The harder the going was, the more I believed I would do it. If you can take that attitude toward yourself, throwing yourself over on the side of yourself when you're overtaken by adversity, or when people are against you, and not go against yourself, then you're using applied faith. You've got to do that.

Maintaining a positive mental attitude and consistently affirming your goals are crucial components of applied faith. The subconscious mind must be trained to attract the outcomes you desire, and this requires unwavering belief and constant reinforcement of your goals. By recognizing the role of Infinite Intelligence and understanding that limitations are self-imposed, you can unlock your full potential. Embrace the philosophy that your mind has no boundaries except those you establish, and leverage this belief to overcome any adversity. Faith, combined with perseverance and self-belief, forms the foundation of achieving remarkable success.

Do you know there are testing times for people? Nobody is permitted to attain a high state in life and stay there without being tested. Nobody is allowed to go into a well-managed business or rise to a high position and stay there without being tested at lower positions until, step-by-step, they earn the right to be on the top. I don't know how the Creator runs his business entirely, but I can catch a pretty good idea of how he does it from observing that part which I can understand. Of course, there's much more that I can't understand, but I can definitely see that he allows nobody to attain a higher stage of life without giving them severe testing.

One of the most outstanding things that I found in my research was that the men of great achievement in all walks of life, and throughout the ages, were great only in proportion to the extent they had been defeated and the opposition they had faced. What an outstanding thing. It couldn't be a coincidence that every one of these outstanding men was exactly great in proportion to how small they had once been, how much they had been opposed, and how intensely they had struggled.

I used to tell of my early struggles and recount some of my defeats. My business manager said it wasn't a good idea. I think it's a fine idea because if you knew the magnitude of the major defeats that I have met, recognizing how I still kept my head above water and still live to deliver this philosophy, you'd say, 'If Hill can do it, I can do it too.' That's the only reason I ever spoke of it.

I don't mind what terms you use: God, Jehovah, Buddha, or Muhammad. You can call it anything you want to. No matter what you call it, we're all talking about one first cause. There aren't two first causes, there's only one. There couldn't be two. There's one first cause that's responsible for this great universe we're living in—for you and for me and for everything that's in the universe. I call it Infinite Intelligence because I have students of all faiths and all religions all over the world and Infinite Intelligence happens to be a neutral term nobody can object to.

These testing times are a critical part of the journey to success. They shape character, build resilience, and develop the necessary skills and wisdom to handle higher responsibilities. The Creator seems to have designed life in such a way that those who aspire to rise must first prove their mettle through trials and tribulations. Observing this pattern in the lives of great achievers, it becomes clear that enduring hardships and overcoming obstacles are prerequisites for attaining true greatness.

The men of great achievement did not reach their pinnacle by accident or luck. They faced numerous setbacks, defeats, and challenges. It is precisely these adversities that tempered their spirits, strengthened their resolve, and honed their abilities. Their greatness is directly proportional to the struggles they endured and the perseverance they demonstrated.

By sharing my own struggles and defeats, I aim to inspire others. Knowing that I faced significant challenges and still succeeded can motivate others to persist in their own endeavors. It is a reminder that setbacks are not the end but rather stepping stones to success. If I can overcome adversity, so can you.

In recognizing a single first cause, whether you call it God, Jehovah, Buddha, Muhammad, or Infinite Intelligence, we acknowledge a universal source of order and purpose. This understanding transcends individual beliefs and unites us in the recognition of a higher power that guides and sustains the universe. By embracing this concept, we can draw strength and inspiration from a profound sense of connection to the infinite and the divine.

But unless you not only believe in that, but can also prove to yourself, and absolutely put down on paper evidence that there is a first cause that you can draw upon, you're not going to be able to make the fullest use of a definite plan. One of my students asked me about my concept of Infinite Intelligence and if I meant the same thing as God. I said, 'Yes, I do.' 'Well,' he said, 'can you prove the existence of your concept of God?' I replied, 'Everything in the universe is the finest evidence of Its existence, because of the orderliness of the universe.'

Everything's orderly, from the electrons and protons in the smallest part of the matter up to the largest suns that float through the heavens. Everything's in orderliness: no chaos, no running together of the planets. There's more evidence of a first cause than there is of anything that I know of. And, if you don't believe that, if you don't accept it, if you don't see it, if you don't feel it, and if you don't know it, then you won't know that you are a minute part of that Infinite Intelligence being expressed through your brain. If you recognize that, then you recognize the truth of what I said—that your only limitations are those which you set up in your mind, or permit somebody to set up there, or let circumstances establish there for you.

A careful inventory of your past defeats and the adversities arising from them shows that all such experiences do carry the seed of an equivalent benefit. Reflect on your own experiences and see how each setback carried within it the potential for growth, learning, and eventual success. This principle is not just a comforting thought but a practical approach to dealing with life's challenges.

Believing in a higher power, or Infinite Intelligence, is crucial. This belief provides a foundation for faith and a framework for understanding the order and purpose in the universe. By acknowledging this higher power, you can tap into a source of strength and guidance that transcends individual limitations. This connection to Infinite Intelligence empowers you to overcome obstacles and achieve your goals.

Your mind, as a part of this Infinite Intelligence, has no inherent limitations. The only boundaries are those you set for yourself or allow others to impose upon you. By recognizing and embracing this truth, you can break free from self-imposed constraints and realize your full potential. This shift in mindset is essential for making the fullest use of a definite plan and achieving your major purpose in life.

Moreover, understanding and accepting the concept of a higher power provides a sense of purpose and direction. It helps you see the bigger picture and understand that your struggles and adversities are part of a larger plan. This perspective allows you to remain steadfast in the face of challenges, knowing that each difficulty carries the seed of an equivalent benefit. To truly harness the power of applied faith, you must internalize these principles and integrate them into your daily life. Affirm your definite major purpose regularly, recognize the role of Infinite Intelligence, and take an inventory of your past defeats to uncover the benefits they have brought you. By doing so, you align yourself with the natural order of the universe and position yourself for success.

In conclusion, applied faith is not just about belief; it requires action, affirmation, and a deep understanding of the principles that govern success. By acknowledging a higher power, affirming your goals, and learning from past adversities, you can unlock the full potential of your mind and achieve your greatest aspirations. This approach empowers you to navigate life's challenges with confidence and resilience, transforming setbacks into stepping stones on the path to success.

PART II

Navigating the Road to Success

Objects do not offer, without object which permits us to act, then validity, the most serious resolutions would soon become nothing but vague projects, destined soon to founder.

It confounds also art the cause and the object of things

... is coming span which causes an avatar that difference that few persons are willing to accept, and which are between judgement and opinion.

... also never succeed in exactly confounding facts, and from this mistake results a less frequent cause of failure.

Opinion is a .... determination nearly general, ...

In addition to this, as it is based on metaphysics, truth and probability, it is rarely free from the personal element.

Opinion depends upon the favourite inclination, upon the mood of the moment, upon sundry considerations, which direct it also, always toward the desired solution.

Also it depends often on thoughtfulness or on the inexactness of the initial representation, which we are pleased to disguise slightly at first, then little by little, to colour in accordance with our desire.

Falsehood does not necessarily enter into this process of tricking things: it is, three quarters of the time, the result of an illusion which we are prone to perpetuate within us.

We are too often in the position of the grave wise men who, while ruminating in an old sarcophagus, discovered a vase whose primitive filiation they were unable to determine with any certainty.

One of them was a poet and an idealist. The second only prized positive things.

3

Rocking Your Own Boat

Skepticism is the deadly enemy of progress and self-development. You might as well lay this book aside and stop right here if you approach this lesson with the feeling that it was written by some long-haired theorist who had never tested the principles upon which the lesson is based. Surely, this is no age for the skeptic, because it is an age in which we have seen more of nature's laws uncovered and harnessed than had been discovered in all past history of the human race.

Within three decades, we have witnessed the mastery of the air; we have explored the ocean; we have all but annihilated distances on the earth; we have harnessed the lightning and made it turn the wheels of industry; we have made seven blades of grass grow where but one grew before; we have instantaneous communication between the nations of the world. Truly, this is an age of illumination and unfoldment, but we have as yet barely scratched the surface of knowledge. However, when we shall have unlocked the gate that leads to the secret power which is stored up within us, it will bring us knowledge that will make all past discoveries pale into oblivion by comparison.

Thought is the most highly organized form of energy known to man, and this is an age of experimentation and research that is sure to bring us into greater understanding of that mysterious force called thought, which reposes within us. We have already found out enough about the human mind to know that a man may throw off the accumulated effects of a thousand generations of fear through the aid of the principle of auto-suggestion. We have already discovered the fact that fear is the chief reason for poverty and failure and misery, which takes on a thousand different forms. We have already discovered the fact that the man who masters fear may march on to successful achievement in practically any undertaking, despite all efforts to defeat him.

This age is characterized by remarkable progress and unprecedented discoveries, revealing the vast potential of human ingenuity and the limitless possibilities that lie ahead. We are living in a time where skepticism can hinder our advancement, as it closes the mind to the incredible breakthroughs that have transformed our world. From the mastery of the skies to the depths of the oceans, from the conquest of vast distances to the harnessing of electricity, our achievements are a testament to the power of human thought and determination.

Yet, despite these advancements, we are only beginning to understand the true potential of the human mind. Thought, the most highly organized form of energy, holds the key to unlocking even greater discoveries. Through experimentation and research, we are on the brink of a deeper comprehension of this mysterious force that resides within each of us. The principle of auto-suggestion has already shown us that we can overcome the ingrained fears of countless generations, breaking free from the chains that bind us to poverty, failure, and misery.

Fear, as we have come to understand, is the primary obstacle to success and happiness. It manifests in myriad forms, but its essence remains the same: it is a barrier that prevents us from realizing our true potential. However, those who conquer fear can achieve extraordinary success, regardless of the challenges they face. The ability to master fear and harness the power of thought is a fundamental principle that can propel individuals toward their goals, enabling them to achieve what might have once seemed impossible.

This is not a time for skepticism but for open-minded exploration and belief in the boundless capabilities of the human spirit. By embracing the principles of faith, positive thinking, and the power of the mind, we can continue to make strides that will dwarf all past achievements. The journey of self-discovery and development is one that requires courage, determination, and an unwavering belief in the potential that lies within us all.

The development of self-confidence starts with the elimination of this demon called fear, which sits upon a man's shoulder and whispers into his ear, 'You can't do it—you are afraid to try—you are afraid of public opinion—you are afraid that you will fail—you are afraid you have not the ability.' This fear demon is getting into close quarters. Science has found a deadly weapon with which to put it to flight, and this lesson on self-confidence has brought you this weapon for use in your battle with the world-old enemy of progress, fear.

SIX BASIC FEARS OF MANKIND

Every person falls heir to the influence of six basic fears. Under these six fears may be listed the lesser fears. The six basic or major fears are here enumerated, and the sources from which they are believed to have grown are described. The six basic fears are:

a. The Fear of Poverty
b. The Fear of Old Age
c. The Fear of Criticism
d. The Fear of Loss of Love of Someone
e. The Fear of Ill Health
f. The Fear of Death

Study the list, then take inventory of your own fears and ascertain under which of the six headings you can classify them. Every human being who has reached the age of understanding is bound down, to some extent, by one or more of these six basic fears. As the first step in the elimination of these six evils, let us examine the sources from whence we inherited them.

The fear of poverty is rooted in the instinct of self-preservation, the basic drive to secure the necessities of life. This fear can paralyze ambition and lead to a life of mediocrity, preventing individuals from taking risks or pursuing their dreams. The fear of old age stems from the uncertainty of what lies ahead, the potential loss of health, vitality, and relevance. It can cause individuals to cling to youth or become despondent about the future.

The fear of criticism is deeply embedded in the human psyche, originating from our social nature and the desire to be accepted and approved by others. This fear can stifle creativity and self-expression, leading to conformity and a reluctance to stand out or voice one's true opinions. The fear of loss of love of someone is a powerful emotional force, rooted in our need for connection and affection. It can cause individuals to tolerate toxic relationships or compromise their values to avoid loneliness or rejection.

The fear of ill health is another fundamental fear, driven by the desire to avoid pain and suffering. This fear can lead to excessive worry and anxiety, detracting from the quality of life and potentially manifesting in psychosomatic illnesses. Lastly, the fear of death is the most universal of all, stemming from the unknown and the finality of life's end. This fear can either paralyze individuals or spur them to make the most of their time on earth.

To eliminate these fears, one must first acknowledge and understand their origins. Reflect on your personal experiences and identify which of these fears resonate most strongly with you. Recognizing these fears is the first step towards overcoming them. Use the principle of auto-suggestion to reprogram your subconscious mind, replacing fear with positive affirmations and beliefs about your capabilities and potential.

Furthermore, develop a positive mental attitude by focusing on your strengths and achievements, rather than dwelling on your shortcomings and failures. Surround yourself with supportive and encouraging individuals who believe in your potential and can help you stay motivated. Engage in continuous learning and self-improvement to build your skills and confidence, reducing the power of fear over your life.

Fear is a natural part of the human experience, but it need not control your destiny. By understanding the six basic fears and their origins, you can begin to dismantle their influence over your life. Embrace the principles of self-confidence and positive thinking, and use them as tools to conquer your fears and achieve your goals. The journey towards self-confidence and personal growth is a lifelong endeavor, but with determination and the right mindset, you can overcome any obstacle and live a fulfilling and successful life.

Physical and social heredity are fundamental concepts in understanding the development of human traits, both physical and mental. Physical heredity traces back to the evolutionary journey of man, starting from the amoeba and progressing through various stages that encompass all existing and extinct animal forms on Earth. Each generation has contributed to human nature, incorporating traits, habits, and physical characteristics from its predecessors, resulting in a diverse and complex inheritance.

While physical heredity shapes the physical aspects of humans, social heredity influences the mental and behavioral traits passed down through cultural and societal influences. Unlike physical traits, mental states such as the six basic fears—poverty, old age, criticism, loss of love, ill health, and death—are not transmitted through physical heredity. However, physical heredity provides a fertile ground where these fears can manifest and persist.

The process of physical evolution itself underscores themes of death, destruction, pain, and cruelty. It operates on the principle that life sustains itself through the consumption of other life forms or elements. Plants absorb nutrients from the soil and air, while animals consume other animals or vegetation. This cycle of consumption is integral to the evolutionary process, shaping the intelligence and survival instincts of each organism.

For instance, the intelligence within plant cells and animal cells reflects their adaptation to their environments and interactions with other life forms. Animal cells, having evolved strategies for survival, carry with them the fear and caution learned from their interactions with predators or competitors. This accumulated wisdom, embedded in the genetic and cellular makeup, influences how organisms perceive and respond to threats.

In the case of humans, whose evolutionary history includes hunting and gathering, the cells and genetic predispositions inherited from animal ancestors may contribute to a predisposition towards fear, particularly in contexts where survival instincts are triggered. This phenomenon illustrates how physical heredity not only shapes physical traits but also provides a framework where mental states, such as fear, can find resonance and expression.

Understanding the interplay between physical and social heredity offers insights into the complexities of human behavior and psychology. While physical heredity provides a biological foundation, social heredity—encompassing cultural norms, learned behaviors, and shared experiences—shapes mental attitudes and responses. Together, these factors influence how individuals perceive and navigate the world, highlighting the intricate balance between genetic inheritance and environmental influences in human development.

PHYSICAL AND SOCIAL HEREDITY

Physical and social heredity are fundamental concepts in understanding the development of human traits, both physical and mental. Physical heredity traces back to the evolutionary journey of man, starting from the amoeba and progressing through various stages that encompass all existing and extinct animal forms on Earth. Each generation has contributed to human nature, incorporating traits, habits, and physical characteristics from its predecessors, resulting in a diverse and complex inheritance.

While physical heredity shapes the physical aspects of humans, social heredity influences the mental and behavioral traits passed down through cultural and societal influences. Unlike physical traits, mental states such as the six basic fears—poverty, old age, criticism, loss of love, ill health, and death—are not transmitted through physical heredity. However, physical heredity provides a fertile ground where these fears can manifest and persist.

The process of physical evolution itself underscores themes of death, destruction, pain, and cruelty. It operates on the principle that life sustains itself through the consumption of other life forms or elements. Plants absorb nutrients from the soil and air, while animals consume other animals or vegetation. This cycle of consumption is integral to the evolutionary process, shaping the intelligence and survival instincts of each organism.

For instance, the intelligence within plant cells and animal cells reflects their adaptation to their environments and interactions with other life forms. Animal cells, having evolved strategies for survival, carry with them the fear and caution learned from their interactions with predators or competitors. This accumulated wisdom, embedded in the genetic and cellular makeup, influences how organisms perceive and respond to threats.

In the case of humans, whose evolutionary history includes hunting and gathering, the cells and genetic predispositions inherited from animal ancestors may contribute to a predisposition towards fear, particularly in contexts where survival instincts are triggered. This phenomenon illustrates how physical heredity not only shapes physical traits but also provides a framework where mental states, such as fear, can find resonance and expression.

Understanding the interplay between physical and social heredity offers insights into the complexities of human behavior and psychology. While physical heredity provides a biological foundation, social heredity—encompassing cultural norms, learned behaviors, and shared experiences—shapes mental attitudes and responses. Together, these factors influence how individuals perceive and navigate the world, highlighting the intricate balance between genetic inheritance and environmental influences in human development.

THEORIES OF FEAR: ORIGINS

This theory may appear far-fetched, and indeed, it may lack conclusive proof, yet it stands as a logical hypothesis at the very least. The author does not assert this theory as definitive, nor does he claim it explains the origins of the six basic fears. Another, more compelling explanation for the source of these fears exists, which we will now explore, starting with an examination of Social Heredity.

Social Heredity constitutes the most significant aspect of human composition, governed by the mechanisms through which each generation passes on to the next the superstitions, beliefs, legends, and ideas inherited from preceding generations. This term encompasses all avenues through which an individual acquires knowledge, including formal education, religious teachings, oral traditions, literature, conversations, storytelling, and personal experiences widely accepted as truth.

Through the workings of social heredity, those influencing a child's mind can imbue it with any idea, whether true or false, through intensive teaching. This process embeds the idea so deeply in the child's psyche that it becomes an inseparable part of their personality, akin to any physical cell or organ in their body, and equally resistant to change in its fundamental nature.

Social Heredity and the Implantation of Beliefs

It is through the law of social heredity that religious doctrines, creeds, and rituals are instilled in the impressionable minds of children. Religionists persistently present these ideas to young minds until they are accepted and firmly entrenched as unshakable beliefs.

During the formative years of a child's life, typically the first two years, the mind is receptive and malleable. Any idea introduced by a trusted figure takes root deeply and becomes ingrained, resisting efforts to erase it, even if it defies logic or reason.

Many adherents of religious faiths assert that they can implant their beliefs so deeply that there is no room left in the child's mind for any alternative views. Such claims, though seemingly exaggerated, often hold true in practice.

Understanding this process of social heredity is crucial for examining the origins of the six basic fears inherited by humanity. Interested students, except those hindered by personal superstitions, can validate the validity of social heredity in relation to these fears through their own life experiences.

Thankfully, the evidence presented in this lesson invites sincere seekers of truth to independently verify its validity. This approach ensures that all who genuinely seek understanding can assess the soundness of the principles discussed.

For now, set aside your biases and preconceptions (you can always revisit them later), as we delve into the origin and essence of humanity's six most formidable adversaries, starting with:

The Fear of Poverty

Courage is needed to confront the truth about the genesis of this fear, and perhaps even more courage is required to accept that truth once it is revealed. The fear of poverty stems from humanity's ingrained inclination to economically exploit one another. While lower animals rely on instinct without the capacity for reasoned thought, humans, with their heightened intuition and intellect, refrain from physical predation and instead derive satisfaction from exploiting others financially.

Throughout recorded history, and particularly in the current era, the worship of money appears ubiquitous. A person's worth often seems measured by their wealth, leaving those without substantial financial resources feeling insignificant and undervalued. Poverty brings profound suffering and indignity to humanity, prompting a deep-seated fear among individuals.

Through generations of learned experiences, humanity has discovered through practical examples that one cannot always trust others, particularly when financial matters or material possessions are involved. This awareness has shaped a fear deeply rooted in the human psyche.

It is no surprise that many marriages are initiated and sometimes dissolved based solely on the economic status of the partners involved. Such circumstances contribute significantly to the bustling activity of divorce courts, underscoring the pervasive impact of financial considerations on human relationships.

'Society' could justifiably be renamed 'Society$' given its inseparable association with the dollar sign. Such is humanity's fervor for wealth that individuals will acquire it by any means available—preferably legal, but resorting to other methods if necessary.

The fear of poverty is profoundly distressing! It drives individuals to extreme measures, including acts as heinous as murder, robbery, and other violations of human rights. Shockingly, societal forgiveness often hinges less on the severity of these transgressions than on the perpetrator's ability to retain their wealth. Poverty, therefore, is not merely an economic state but is perceived as a criminal offense—an unforgivable sin in the eyes of society.

It is no wonder that this fear permeates every facet of human life. Legal codes worldwide attest to its pervasive influence, with countless laws aimed at shielding the vulnerable from the powerful.

Attempting to dispute that the fear of poverty is ingrained in human nature or that it arises from mankind's propensity to exploit one another would be as futile as proving that three times two equals six. If trust among individuals were universal, poverty would be virtually unknown. There is ample food, shelter, clothing, and luxuries for every person on Earth, yet humanity's relentless pursuit of wealth often perpetuates scarcity by hoarding resources even beyond personal need.

In summary, the fear of poverty stands as one of humanity's primordial fears, deeply rooted in our societal and economic frameworks, and profoundly shaping our actions and beliefs.

The second of mankind's foundational fears is the fear of old age. This apprehension primarily springs from two distinct sources. Firstly, there is the dread that advancing years may usher in poverty. Secondly, and more significantly, this fear originates from the dissemination of false and oppressive religious doctrines, often intertwined with concepts of 'fire and brimstone,' 'purgatories,' and other terrifying notions. These teachings have instilled a deep-seated fear of old age by portraying it as the harbinger of a potentially even more horrific existence beyond this already troublesome world.

The fear of old age is therefore compounded by two profound concerns. The first is rooted in a profound mistrust of one's fellow human beings, who might exploit the vulnerabilities of the elderly to seize whatever material possessions they have accumulated. The second source of anxiety emerges from the haunting images of an afterlife, which have been ingrained in the human psyche through the pervasive influence of social heredity long before individuals reach maturity.

Given these circumstances, it is entirely understandable why humanity dreads the encroaching years of old age with such intensity.

The Fear of Criticism

The third of mankind's intrinsic fears is the fear of criticism. The precise origins of this fundamental fear are difficult, if not impossible, to definitively pinpoint, but its pervasive presence in human psychology is undeniable.

Some posit that this fear first emerged concurrent with the advent of politics. Others attribute its genesis to the formation of gatherings of women known as 'Woman's Clubs.' Yet another perspective humorously attributes its roots to the vivid and often vehement critiques found within the pages of the Holy Bible. According to this view, if one takes these scriptural criticisms literally, then even God Himself, as the author of the Bible, bears responsibility for implanting in humanity this inherent fear of criticism.

As for this author, not a humorist nor a prophet, but a pragmatic individual of everyday experience, the basic fear of criticism is likely ingrained in the human psyche as part of an inherited propensity. This inclination compels individuals not only to covet the possessions of others but also to justify such actions through the critique of their character.

The fear of criticism manifests itself in myriad forms, often trivial and even childish in nature. For instance, many bald-headed men owe their condition not to natural causes but rather to their fear of criticism. Their baldness often results from wearing hats with tight-fitting bands that constrict blood flow to the hair roots. Men wear these hats not out of necessity but because of societal conformity—fearing criticism if they do not conform.

In contrast, women rarely experience baldness or thinning hair because they wear hats primarily for appearances, opting for styles that are loose and comfortable rather than conforming to societal pressures.

However, it should not be assumed that women are exempt from the fear of criticism when it comes to hats. If any woman claims superiority over men in this regard, challenge her to stroll down the street wearing a hat that is one or two seasons out of fashion!

Manufacturers of all types of clothing have astutely capitalized on this fundamental fear of criticism that afflicts all of humanity. Each season, we observe changes in 'styles' across various articles of apparel. Who dictates these 'styles'? Certainly not the consumers who purchase the clothing, but rather the manufacturers themselves. Why do they alter styles so frequently? Clearly, it's a strategic move to stimulate more sales.

Similarly, most automobile manufacturers (with a few rare and practical exceptions) change their car designs every season for the same reason—to capitalize on the fear ingrained in human nature that recoils from wearing or driving anything deemed outdated by the masses.

The clothing industry understands well how the human-animal dreads wearing garments that are even slightly out of sync with the current fashion trends. Have you not experienced this yourself? Our observations thus far have detailed how people react under the influence of the fear of criticism, particularly in matters concerning trivialities of daily life.

Now, let's delve into how this fear influences human behavior in more significant aspects of social interaction. Consider almost any individual who has reached 'mental maturity' (generally between thirty-five to forty-five years of age), and if you could peer into their thoughts, you would likely find a pronounced skepticism and resistance towards many of the doctrines propagated by mainstream religious teachings. Such is the profound and potent impact of the fear of criticism!

Not long ago, the mere label of 'infidel' could spell ruin for anyone so branded. It becomes evident, therefore, that humanity's fear of criticism is not without substantial justification for its existence.

The Fear of Loss of Love of Someone

The origins of this fear require little elaboration, as it is evident that it stems from humanity's natural inclination towards possessiveness and jealousy, particularly in matters of romantic relationships. Historically, men have shown a predisposition towards polygamy, a fact that is often denied by those who are either no longer sexually active due to age or other reasons that have led to changes in their hormonal balance.

It is widely acknowledged that feelings of jealousy and other related forms of emotional distress, which can be likened to mild forms of insanity, have evolved from this innate fear of losing the affection and loyalty of a loved one.

Among the many peculiar and inexplicable behaviors observed by this author, one of the most perplexing involves individuals who become consumed by jealousy towards their romantic partners. While the author has had only one personal encounter with this form of mental turmoil, it was sufficient to affirm that the fear of losing someone's love ranks among the most agonizing, if not the most agonizing, of all the six fundamental fears. It stands to reason that this fear exerts a more profound and disruptive influence on the human psyche than any of the other fears, often culminating in severe and enduring forms of mental illness.

The Fear of Ill Health

The fifth of humanity's fundamental fears is the fear of ill health. This fear, akin to the fears of poverty and old age, shares common origins and concerns, residing in the realms of perceived afflictions and uncertainties that humanity often dreads.

The author posits a strong suspicion that those engaged in the promotion of health and wellness practices have played a significant role in perpetuating this fear of ill health within the human psyche. Throughout recorded history, various forms of therapies and health practitioners have been prevalent. It stands to reason that individuals who earn their livelihood from advocating for good health would utilize every available means to impress upon people the necessity of their services. This continual reinforcement over time could potentially embed a profound fear of ill health deep within individuals, passed down through successive generations.

Moreover, the fear of ill health is not merely a product of economic interests. It also stems from the inherent vulnerability of human existence. Illness, injury, and the decline of physical well-being are universal experiences that can strike at any time, regardless of one's socioeconomic status. This unpredictability fosters a sense of fear and apprehension about one's health, compelling individuals to seek assurances and remedies, often from healthcare providers and wellness experts who capitalize on these anxieties.

Furthermore, cultural and societal norms contribute to the fear of ill health. Media portrayals, medical advancements, and societal expectations around physical appearance and longevity shape collective attitudes towards health. The relentless pursuit of youthfulness and vitality, coupled with the fear of aging and decline, amplifies anxieties about health. This cultural backdrop reinforces the fear of ill health as a prevalent concern that influences personal decisions, healthcare choices, and societal priorities.

The Fear of Death

The sixth and final of humanity's fundamental fears is the fear of death. This fear stands out as the most dreaded among the six basic fears, a sentiment readily discernible even to the casual observer of psychology.

The intense fear associated with death can be primarily attributed to religious fanaticism, which arguably plays a more significant role in fostering this fear than all other influences combined. Interestingly, so-called 'heathens' often exhibit less fear of death compared to the 'civilized,' particularly those influenced by theological doctrines.

For countless millennia, humans have grappled with unanswered and perhaps unanswerable questions: 'Where did I come from, and where will I go after death?' The quest for answers has spurred a variety of responses from both cunning manipulators and sincere believers. This pursuit has even become a so-called 'learned' profession, despite requiring minimal actual learning. Herein lies a major source of the fear of death.

Religious leaders, in their quest to attract followers and secure authority, have offered assurances and warnings regarding the afterlife. 'Join my congregation, embrace my beliefs, adhere to my doctrines (and contribute to my livelihood), and I will provide you with a ticket straight to heaven upon your demise,' declares one form of sectarianism. Conversely, the same leader warns, 'Stay away from my congregation, and you risk eternal damnation in hell.'

While these self-proclaimed leaders may lack the ability

to grant passage to heaven or condemn someone to eternal torment, the mere prospect of such consequences grips the mind and engenders the fear of death—a fear so profound that it eclipses all others.

The fear of death finds its origins in the deep-seated human desire for answers about existence and the afterlife. Religious teachings and doctrines, often wielded with authority and conviction, amplify this fear, instilling dread and uncertainty in the minds of believers and non-believers alike. Thus, the fear of death remains an enduring aspect of human psychology, influencing beliefs, behaviors, and societal attitudes towards mortality.

In truth, no man knows, and no man has ever known, what heaven or hell is like, or if such places even exist. This very lack of definite knowledge opens the door of the human mind to the charlatan, who seizes the opportunity to enter and control that mind with his stock of legerdemain and various brands of trickery, deceit, and fraud. This much is the truth—nothing less and nothing more—That NO MAN KNOWS, NOR HAS ANY MAN EVER KNOWN, WHERE WE COME FROM AT BIRTH OR WHERE WE GO AT DEATH. Any person claiming otherwise is either deceiving himself or is a conscious impostor who makes it his business to live without rendering a service of value by playing upon the credulity of humanity.

WORDS OF WISDOM FOR THE WIVES

I am going to digress here and break the line of thought for a moment while recording a word of advice specifically for the wives of men. Remember, these lines are intended only for wives, and husbands are not expected to read what is set down here.

From having analyzed more than 16,000 people, the majority of whom were married men, I have learned something that may be of great value to wives. Let me state my thought in these words:

You have it within your power to send your husband away to his work, business, or profession each day with a feeling of self-confidence that will carry him successfully over the rough spots of the day and bring him home again, at night, smiling and happy. One of my acquaintances from former years married a woman who had a set of false teeth. One day, his wife dropped her teeth and broke the plate. The husband picked up the pieces and began examining them. He showed such interest in them that his wife said:

> 'You could make a set of teeth like those if you made up your mind to do it.'

This man was a farmer whose ambitions had never carried him beyond the bounds of his little farm until his wife made that remark. She walked over, laid her hand on his shoulder, and encouraged him to try his hand at dentistry. She finally coaxed him to make the start, and today, he is one of the most prominent and successful dentists in the state of Virginia. I know him well, for he is my father!

No one can foretell the possibilities of achievement available to the man whose wife stands at his back and urges him on to bigger and better endeavors. It is a well-known fact that a woman can inspire a man to perform almost superhuman feats. It is your right and your duty to encourage your husband and urge him on in worthy undertakings until he finds his place in the world. You have the unique ability to induce him to put forth greater effort than any other person in the world. By making him believe that nothing within reason is beyond his power of achievement, you will have rendered him a service that will significantly help him win the battle of life.

One of the most successful men in his field in America credits his entire success to his wife. When they were first married, she wrote a creed which he signed and placed over his desk. This is a copy of the creed:

> *I believe in myself. I believe in those who work with me. I believe in my employer. I believe in my friends. I believe in my family. I believe that God will lend me everything I need with which to succeed if I do my best to earn it through faithful and honest service. I believe in prayer and I will never close my eyes in sleep without praying for divine guidance to the end that I will be patient with other people and tolerant with those who do not believe as I do. I believe that success is the result of intelligent effort and does not depend upon luck or sharp practices or double-crossing friends, fellow men or my employer.*
>
> *I believe I will get out of life exactly what I put into it> therefore I will be careful to conduct myself toward others as I would want them to act toward me. I will not slander those whom I do not like. I will not slight my work no matter what I may see others doing. I will render the best service of which I am capable because I have pledged myself to succeed in life and I know that success is always the result of conscientious and efficient effort. Finally, I will forgive those who offend me because I realise that I shall sometimes offend others and I will need their forgiveness.*

Signed..

The woman who wrote this creed was a practical psychologist of the first order. With the influence and guidance of such a woman as a helpmate, any man could achieve noteworthy success. Analyze this creed and you will notice how freely the personal pronoun is used. It starts off with the affirmation of self-confidence, which is perfectly proper. No man could make this creed his own without developing the positive attitude that would attract to him people who would aid him in his struggle for success.

This would be a splendid creed for every salesman to adopt. It might not hurt your chances for success if you adopted it. Mere adoption, however, is not enough. You must practice it! Read it over and over until you know it by heart. Then repeat it at least once a day until you have literally transformed it into your mental makeup. Keep a copy of it before you as a daily reminder of your pledge to practice it. By doing so, you will be making efficient use of the principle of auto-suggestion as a means of developing self-confidence. Never mind what anyone may say about your procedure. Just remember that it is your business to succeed, and this creed, if mastered and applied, will go a long way toward helping you achieve that success.

You might well remember that nothing can bring you success but yourself. Of course, you will need the cooperation of others if you aim to attain success of a far-reaching nature, but you will never get that cooperation unless you vitalize your mind with the positive attitude of self-confidence.

We come now to the point at which you are ready to take hold of the principle of auto-suggestion and make direct use of it in developing yourself into a positive, dynamic, and self-reliant person. You are instructed to copy the following formula, sign it, and commit it to memory:

SELF-CONFIDENCE FORMULA

First: I know that I have the ability to achieve the object of my definite purpose. Therefore, I demand of myself persistent, aggressive, and continuous action toward its attainment. I am aware that consistent effort and determination are key to reaching my goals, and I will not allow obstacles to deter me from my path.

Second: I realize that the dominating thoughts of my mind eventually reproduce themselves in outward, bodily action, and gradually transform themselves into physical reality. Therefore, I will concentrate my mind for thirty minutes daily upon the task of thinking of the person I intend to be. By creating a vivid mental picture of this person, I will then transform that picture into reality through practical service. This practice will help me align my thoughts and actions with my desired outcomes.

Third: I know that through the principle of auto suggestion, any desire that I persistently hold in my mind will eventually seek expression through some practical means of realizing it. Therefore, I shall devote ten minutes daily to demanding of myself the development of the factors named in the sixteen lessons of this Reading Course on the Law of Success. This commitment will help me internalize and apply these principles effectively.

Fourth: I have clearly mapped out and written down a detailed description of my definite purpose in life for the coming five years. I have set a specific price on my services for each of these five years; a price that I intend to earn and receive through strict application of the principle of efficient, satisfactory service, which I will render in advance. By doing so, I will ensure that my efforts are well-compensated and aligned with my goals.

Fifth: I fully realize that no wealth or position can long endure unless built upon truth and justice. Therefore, I will engage in no transaction that does not benefit all whom it affects. I will succeed by attracting to me the forces I wish to use and the cooperation of other people. I will induce others to serve me because I will first serve them. I will eliminate hatred, envy, jealousy, selfishness, and cynicism by developing love for all humanity because I know that a negative attitude toward others can never bring me success. I will cause others to believe in me because I will believe in them and in myself.

I will sign my name to this formula, commit it to memory, and repeat it aloud once a day with full faith that it will gradually influence my entire life. By doing so, I will become a successful and happy worker in my chosen field of endeavor.

Signed ....

Before you sign your name to this formula, make sure that you genuinely intend to carry out its instructions. Behind this formula lies a law that no man can fully explain. Psychologists refer to this law as auto-suggestion and leave it at that. However, you should bear in mind one undeniable fact: whatever this law is, it actually works!

Another important point to keep in mind is the fact that, just as electricity can turn the wheels of industry and serve mankind in a million other ways—or snuff out life if wrongly applied—so will this principle of auto-suggestion lead you up the mountainside of peace and prosperity or down into the valley of misery and poverty, depending on how you apply it.

If you fill your mind with doubt and unbelief in your ability to achieve, then the principle of auto-suggestion takes this spirit of unbelief, sets it up in your subconscious mind as your dominating thought, and slowly but surely draws you into the whirlpool of failure. But, if you fill your mind with radiant self-confidence, the principle of auto-suggestion takes this belief, sets it up as your dominating thought, and helps you master the obstacles that fall in your way until you reach the mountaintop of success.

Remember, the way you choose to apply this principle will determine your outcome. If you wholeheartedly embrace self-confidence and believe in your abilities, auto-suggestion will reinforce this belief, empowering you to overcome challenges and achieve your goals. On the other hand, if you allow doubt and negativity to dominate your thoughts, auto-suggestion will reinforce these limiting beliefs and hinder your progress. Therefore, it is crucial to consciously cultivate positive and empowering thoughts, ensuring that auto-suggestion works in your favor, propelling you toward success and fulfillment.

THE POWER OF HABIT

Having, myself, experienced all the difficulties that stand in the road of those who lack the understanding to make practical application of this great principle of auto-suggestion, let me take you a short way into the principle of habit. Through the aid of habit, you may easily apply the principle of auto-suggestion in any direction and for any purpose whatsoever.

Habit grows out of environment; it develops from doing the same thing, thinking the same thoughts, or repeating the same words over and over again. Habit may be likened to the groove on a phonograph record, while the human mind may be likened to the needle that fits into that groove. When any habit has been well-formed through repetition of thought or action, the mind has a tendency to attach itself to and follow the course of that habit as closely as the phonograph needle follows the groove in the wax record.

Habit is created by repeatedly directing one or more of the five senses of seeing, hearing, smelling, tasting, and feeling in a given direction. It is through this repetition principle that the injurious drug habit is formed. It is through this same principle that the desire for intoxicating drink is formed into a habit.

Habits can be both constructive and destructive. Just as negative habits such as drug addiction and alcohol dependency are formed through repeated exposure and reinforcement, positive habits can be cultivated in the same manner. By consciously directing your thoughts and actions towards positive and beneficial outcomes, you can form habits that support your goals and aspirations.

To harness the power of habit for your benefit, begin by identifying the thoughts and actions that align with your desired outcomes. Then, through consistent repetition and reinforcement, these thoughts and actions will gradually become ingrained as habits. Over time, your mind will naturally follow these positive habits, much like the needle of a phonograph record follows its groove. This process will make it easier for you to maintain the positive behaviors and attitudes that contribute to your success and well-being.

Remember, the formation of habits, whether positive or negative, is a result of repeated actions and thoughts. By deliberately choosing to focus on positive, empowering habits, you can effectively use the principle of auto-suggestion to shape your life in a meaningful and fulfilling way.

After habit has been well established, it will automatically control and direct our bodily activity. Within this realization lies a thought that can be transformed into a powerful factor in the development of self-confidence. The thought is this: voluntarily, and by force if necessary, direct your efforts and your thoughts along a desired line until you have formed the habit that will take hold of you and continue, voluntarily, to direct your efforts along the same line.

The object in writing out and repeating the self-confidence formula is to form the habit of making belief in yourself the dominating thought of your mind until that thought has been thoroughly embedded in your subconscious mind through the principle of habit.

You learned to write by repeatedly directing the muscles of your arm and hand over certain outlines known as letters until, finally, you formed the habit of tracing these outlines. Now you write with ease and rapidity, without tracing each letter slowly. Writing has become a habit for you.

The principle of habit will take hold of the faculties of your mind just as it will influence the physical muscles of your body, as you can easily prove by mastering and applying this lesson on self-confidence. Any statement that you repeatedly make to yourself, or any desire that you deeply plant in your mind through repeated statements, will eventually seek expression through your physical, outward bodily efforts. The principle of habit is the very foundation upon which this lesson on self-confidence is built. If you understand and follow the directions laid down in this lesson, you will soon know more about the law of habit from firsthand knowledge than could be taught by a thousand such lessons as this.

You have but little conception of the possibilities that lie sleeping within you, awaiting but the awakening hand of vision to arouse you. You will never have a better conception of those possibilities unless you develop sufficient self-confidence to lift you above the commonplace influences of your present environment.

Realize that habit, once established, guides both physical and mental actions. By consciously forming positive habits, you can direct your thoughts and efforts towards your desired goals. The practice of writing and repeating the self-confidence formula is aimed at embedding a strong belief in yourself into your subconscious mind. Just as you mastered the skill of writing through repeated practice, you can master the development of self-confidence by consistently focusing on positive thoughts and actions.

Remember, the principle of habit operates both in your physical actions and in the faculties of your mind. By diligently applying the lessons of self-confidence and understanding the law of habit, you can unlock and realize the immense potential within you. This potential is awaiting the moment when you develop the vision and self-confidence to rise above the ordinary influences of your current surroundings and achieve extraordinary success.

The human mind is a marvelous, mysterious piece of machinery, a fact of which I was reminded a few months ago when I picked up Emerson's Essays and re-read his essay on Spiritual Laws. A strange thing happened. I saw in that essay, which I had read scores of times previously, much that I had never noticed before. I saw more in this essay than I had seen during previous readings because the unfoldment of my mind since the last reading had prepared me to interpret more.

The human mind is constantly unfolding, like the petals of a flower, until it reaches the maximum of development. What this maximum is, where it ends, or whether it ends at all or not, are unanswerable questions, but the degree of unfoldment seems to vary according to the nature of the individual and the degree to which he keeps his mind at work. A mind that is forced or coaxed into analytical thought every day seems to keep on unfolding and developing greater powers of interpretation.

Down in Louisville, Kentucky, lives Mr. Lee Cook, a man

who has practically no legs and has to wheel himself around on a cart. In spite of the fact that Mr. Cook has been without legs since birth, he is the owner of a great industry and a millionaire through his own efforts. He has proved that a man can get along very well without legs if he has well-developed self-confidence.

In the city of New York, one may see a strong, able-bodied, and able-headed young man without legs rolling himself down Fifth Avenue every afternoon, with cap in hand, begging for a living. His head is perhaps as sound and as able to think as the average.

This comparison between Mr. Lee Cook and the young beggar in New York highlights the vast difference that self-confidence and a well-developed mind can make in a person's life. Despite their physical limitations, individuals with a strong sense of self-worth and determination can achieve remarkable success. Mr. Cook's example demonstrates that physical limitations do not define one's potential; instead, it is the strength of the mind and the power of self-confidence that determine the extent of one's achievements.

In contrast, the young man begging on Fifth Avenue, though physically capable and mentally sound, lacks the self-confidence and drive that could propel him toward success. This disparity underscores the importance of nurturing and developing the mind. It is through continuous learning, persistent effort, and a positive mindset that one can overcome obstacles and reach their full potential.

Thus, the human mind, when nurtured and developed, can achieve extraordinary feats. The unfoldment of the mind is a lifelong process, influenced by one's environment, experiences, and determination to grow. By fostering self-confidence and engaging in analytical thought, individuals can unlock their hidden potential and accomplish great things, regardless of their physical circumstances.

This young man could achieve everything that Mr. Cook of Louisville has accomplished if he viewed himself through the same lens as Mr. Cook views himself. Henry Ford, who owns more millions of dollars than he will ever need or use, started out as a laborer in a machine shop with minimal schooling and no capital. Despite working alongside many others with potentially better-developed brains, Ford discarded any sense of poverty consciousness, built confidence in his abilities, focused on success, and ultimately achieved it. Had his colleagues adopted his mindset, they could have achieved similar success.

Milo C. Jones, from Wisconsin, was struck down by paralysis a few years ago, rendering him unable to move or turn in bed. Despite his physical limitations, his brain remained unaffected and began functioning with newfound determination. From his bed, Mr. Jones formulated a clear purpose: to produce pork sausage. He gathered his family, outlined his plans, and directed them in executing his vision. With nothing but a sound mind and abundant self-confidence, Milo C. Jones transformed 'Little Pig Sausage' into a renowned brand across the United States, amassing a fortune in the process—achievements made after paralysis had rendered him unable to work physically.

These stories underscore a powerful truth: where there is thought, there is power! Henry Ford's ongoing success stems from his unwavering belief in himself, which he translated into a definitive purpose supported by a concrete plan. In contrast, his fellow machinists envisioned nothing beyond their weekly paychecks and consequently never ventured beyond routine expectations. If you aspire to achieve more, it is imperative to demand more from yourself. Importantly, this demand must originate from within.

The lesson is clear: your mindset and belief in yourself determine your potential for success. By cultivating self-confidence, setting clear goals, and devising actionable plans, you can overcome any adversity and achieve remarkable feats. These examples demonstrate that with the right mindset and determination, individuals can surpass physical limitations and achieve greatness. Thus, the key lies not in external circumstances but in your internal beliefs and the expectations you set for yourself.

4

Fueling Success with Passion

Enthusiasm is a state of mind that inspires and arouses one to put action into the task at hand. It does more than this—it is contagious, and vitally affects not only the enthusiast but all with whom he comes in contact. Enthusiasm bears the same relationship to a human being that steam does to the locomotive—it is the vital moving force that impels action.

The greatest leaders of men are those who know how to inspire enthusiasm in their followers. Enthusiasm is the most important factor entering into salesmanship. It is, by far, the most vital factor that enters into public speaking. It is the spark that ignites passion and drive in others, encouraging them to believe in a vision and to act on it. Without enthusiasm, even the most brilliant ideas can fall flat, failing to capture the interest or commitment of others.

If you wish to understand the difference between a man who is enthusiastic and one who is not, compare Billy Sunday with the average man of his profession. The finest sermon ever delivered would fall upon deaf ears if it were not backed with enthusiasm by the speaker. Enthusiasm gives life to words, making them resonate with the audience and leaving a lasting impact. It is the energy that turns mere communication into a powerful force that can move hearts and minds.

Consider how enthusiasm can transform everyday interactions and professional endeavors. In salesmanship, an enthusiastic salesperson is more likely to persuade and connect with potential customers, creating a sense of excitement and urgency around the product or service being offered. Enthusiasm builds trust and rapport, making others more receptive to the message being conveyed.

In public speaking, enthusiasm captivates the audience, holding their attention and making the delivery memorable. It conveys the speaker's passion and conviction, inspiring listeners to share in the vision and take action. A speaker without enthusiasm may present the same information, but it will lack the emotional impact needed to truly engage and motivate the audience.

Enthusiasm is not just an outward display of energy; it is a genuine internal state that reflects a deep-seated belief in what one is doing. It cannot be faked or forced; true enthusiasm comes from within and is a natural expression of one's commitment and passion. It is this authentic enthusiasm that resonates most powerfully with others, creating a ripple effect that can inspire and drive collective effort toward a common goal.

Therefore, cultivating enthusiasm is essential for anyone who wishes to lead, inspire, or persuade others. It is a key ingredient in the recipe for success, transforming ordinary efforts into extraordinary achievements. Whether in personal or professional contexts, enthusiasm has the power to elevate performance, foster collaboration, and drive meaningful change. By embracing and expressing genuine enthusiasm, you can unlock your potential and influence others in profound ways.

HOW ENTHUSIASM WILL AFFECT YOU

Mix enthusiasm with your work and it will not seem hard or monotonous. Enthusiasm will so energize your entire body that you can get along with less than half the usual amount of sleep and at the same time it will enable you to perform from two to three times as much work as you usually perform in a given period, without fatigue.

For many years I have done most of my writing at night. One night, while I was enthusiastically at work over my typewriter, I looked out of the window of my study, just across the square from the Metropolitan tower in New York City, and saw what seemed to be the most peculiar reflection of the moon on the tower. It was of a silvery gray shade, such as I had never seen before. Upon closer inspection, I found that the reflection was that of the early morning sun and not that of the moon. It was daylight! I had been at work all night, but I was so engrossed in my work that the night had passed as though it were but an hour. I worked at my task all that day and all the following night without stopping, except for a small amount of light food.

Two nights and one day without sleep, and with but little food, without the slightest evidence of fatigue, would not have been possible had I not kept my body energized with enthusiasm over the work at hand. Enthusiasm is not merely a figure of speech; it is a vital force that you can harness and use with profit. Without it you would resemble an electric battery without electricity. Enthusiasm is the vital force with which you recharge your body and develop a dynamic personality.

Some people are blessed with natural enthusiasm, while others must acquire it. The procedure through which it may be developed is simple. It begins by the doing of the work or rendering of the service which one likes best. If you should be so situated that you cannot conveniently engage in the work which you like best, for the time being, then you can proceed along another line very effectively by adopting a definite chief aim that contemplates your engaging in that particular work at some future time.

Enthusiasm will also affect your interactions with others. It has a magnetic quality that attracts people to you, making them more willing to listen, cooperate, and be influenced by your ideas and actions. When you approach tasks with enthusiasm, it becomes infectious, spreading to those around you and creating a positive, energetic environment. This collective enthusiasm can lead to improved teamwork, increased productivity, and a more harmonious work atmosphere.

Moreover, enthusiasm can significantly impact your personal growth and development. It encourages a proactive attitude, prompting you to seek out new opportunities, learn new skills, and overcome challenges with a positive mindset. Enthusiasm fuels perseverance, helping you to stay committed to your goals even when faced with setbacks or obstacles. It transforms ordinary efforts into extraordinary achievements by infusing them with passion and determination.

To cultivate enthusiasm, start by identifying what truly excites and motivates you. Focus on your strengths and interests, and find ways to incorporate them into your daily activities. Set clear, meaningful goals that align with your passions, and remind yourself regularly of the reasons why these goals matter to you. Surround yourself with positive influences, including people who inspire and encourage you. Practice gratitude and celebrate your successes, no matter how small, to maintain a positive and enthusiastic outlook.

Lack of capital and many other circumstances over which you have no immediate control may force you to engage in work which you do not like, but no one can stop you from determining in your own mind what your definite chief aim in life shall be, nor can anyone stop you from planning ways and means for translating this aim into reality, nor can anyone stop you from mixing enthusiasm with your plans.

Happiness, the final object of all human effort, is a state of mind that can be maintained only through the hope of future achievement. Happiness lies always in the future and never in the past. The happy person is the one who dreams of heights of achievement that are yet unattained. The home you intend to own, the money you intend to earn and place in the bank, the trip you intend to take when you can afford it, the position in life you intend to fill when you have prepared yourself, and the preparation, itself—these are the things that produce happiness. Likewise, these are the materials out of which your definite chief aim is formed; these are the things over which you may become enthusiastic, no matter what your present station in life may be.

More than twenty years ago I became enthusiastic over an idea. When the idea first took form in my mind I was unprepared to take even the first step toward its transformation into reality. But I nursed it in my mind—I became enthusiastic over it as I looked ahead, in my imagination, and saw the time when I would be prepared to make it a reality.

I visualized the steps I would take, the obstacles I might encounter, and the ultimate success I would achieve. This enthusiasm fueled my daily actions and kept me focused on my goal, despite the challenges I faced. I read books, sought advice from knowledgeable individuals, and continuously refined my plans. With each passing day, my confidence grew, and so did my resolve to see my idea come to fruition.

Through this process, I learned the importance of patience and persistence. I understood that great achievements are not realized overnight but require consistent effort and unwavering determination. The enthusiasm I had for my idea kept me motivated and resilient, even during times of doubt and difficulty.

Eventually, the time came when I was ready to take concrete steps toward transforming my idea into reality. By then, I had equipped myself with the necessary knowledge, skills, and resources. The enthusiasm that had once been merely a spark of inspiration had grown into a driving force that propelled me forward.

As I embarked on this journey, I encountered both successes and setbacks. However, my enthusiasm never waned. It continued to be the fuel that energized my efforts and kept me moving forward. I found joy in the process of working towards my goal, knowing that each step brought me closer to my ultimate vision.

Today, that idea, which once existed only in my mind, has become a reality. It stands as a testament to the power of enthusiasm and the importance of maintaining a positive and hopeful outlook. My journey has taught me that no matter the obstacles we face, we have the power to shape our destiny through the force of our enthusiasm and determination.

While external circumstances may limit your current options, they cannot restrict your ability to dream, plan, and pursue your definite chief aim. Happiness is found in the pursuit of future achievements, and enthusiasm is the key that unlocks the door to success. By nurturing your dreams with enthusiasm, you can transform them into reality, no matter where you start or what challenges you encounter along the way.

The idea was this: I wanted to become the editor of a magazine, based upon the Golden Rule, through which I could inspire people to keep up courage and deal with one another squarely. I envisioned a publication that would be a beacon of hope, integrity, and encouragement, touching the lives of countless readers. Finally, my chance came! On Armistice Day, 1918, I wrote the first editorial for what was to become the material realization of a hope that had lain dormant in my mind for nearly a score of years.

With enthusiasm, I poured into that editorial the emotions which I had been developing in my heart over a period of more than twenty years. My dream had come true. My editorship of a national magazine had become a reality. As I have stated, this editorial was written with enthusiasm. I took it to a man of my acquaintance and with enthusiasm, I read it to him. The editorial ended in these words: 'At last, my twenty-year-old dream is about to come true. It takes money, and a lot of it, to publish a national magazine, and I haven't the slightest idea where I am going to get this essential factor, but this is worrying me not at all because I know I am going to get it somewhere!' As I wrote those lines, I mixed enthusiasm and faith with them.

I had hardly finished reading this editorial when the man to whom I read it—the first and only person to whom I had shown it—said: 'I can tell you where you are going to get the money, for I am going to supply it.' And he did!

Yes, enthusiasm is a vital force; so vital, in fact, that no man who has it highly developed can begin even to approximate his power of achievement. Enthusiasm not only propels individuals toward their goals but also attracts the support and resources necessary to achieve those goals. It is a magnetic force that draws like-minded people and opportunities, creating a powerful synergy that accelerates progress and success.

The journey of transforming my dream into reality taught me that enthusiasm is more than just a state of mind; it is a dynamic and influential energy that can shape one's destiny. It acts as a catalyst, turning aspirations into tangible outcomes, and infuses every effort with a sense of purpose and vigor. My experience is a testament to the fact that when you embrace your goals with unwavering enthusiasm, you unlock a reservoir of potential within yourself that is capable of overcoming any obstacle.

In reflecting on this journey, I realize that the power of enthusiasm extends beyond personal achievements. It has the capacity to inspire others, ignite collective efforts, and create a ripple effect of positive change. When you approach life with genuine enthusiasm, you become a source of inspiration and motivation for those around you, encouraging them to pursue their own dreams with the same fervor and dedication.

Therefore, I urge you to harness the power of enthusiasm in your own life. Let it be the driving force behind your ambitions, the spark that fuels your perseverance, and the beacon that guides you through challenges. By doing so, you will not only achieve your own goals but also contribute to a world where enthusiasm and positive energy are the norms, leading to greater collective progress and fulfillment.

Before passing to the next step in this lesson, I wish to repeat and to emphasize the fact that you may develop enthusiasm over your definite chief aim in life, no matter whether you are in a position to achieve that purpose at this time or not. You may be a long way from the realization of your definite chief aim, but if you will kindle the fire of enthusiasm in your heart, and keep it burning, before very long the obstacles that now stand in the way of your attainment of that purpose will melt away as if by the force of magic, and you will find yourself in possession of power that you did not know you possessed.

HOW YOUR ENTHUSIASM WILL AFFECT OTHERS

We come, now, to the discussion of one of the most important subjects of this reading course, namely, suggestion. In the preceding lessons, we have discussed the subject of auto-suggestion, which is self-suggestion. You saw, in Lesson Three, what an important part auto-suggestion played. Suggestion is the principle through which your words and your acts and even your state of mind influence others.

When a public speaker 'senses' the feeling that his audience is 'en rapport' with him he merely recognizes the fact that his own enthusiasm has influenced the minds of his listeners until their minds are vibrating in harmony with his own. This harmonious vibration is what creates a bond between the speaker and the audience, allowing for the effective communication of ideas and emotions. The speaker's enthusiasm acts as a catalyst, triggering similar feelings and thoughts in the audience, thereby amplifying the impact of the message being delivered.

The influence of enthusiasm extends beyond public speaking. It plays a crucial role in every aspect of human interaction. For example, in salesmanship, a salesperson who is genuinely enthusiastic about the product they are selling can significantly increase the likelihood of making a sale. Their enthusiasm not only highlights the benefits of the product but also instills a sense of trust and confidence in the buyer. The buyer, in turn, is more likely to respond positively because the salesperson's enthusiasm has created a favorable impression.

In leadership, enthusiasm is an indispensable quality. A leader who approaches their role with enthusiasm can inspire their team to achieve remarkable results. Enthusiastic leaders create an environment where team members feel motivated and valued. This positive atmosphere encourages creativity, productivity, and a willingness to go the extra mile. The leader's enthusiasm acts as a driving force, propelling the entire team toward the achievement of common goals.

Even in personal relationships, enthusiasm plays a vital role. Expressing genuine enthusiasm in interactions with family and friends strengthens bonds and fosters a sense of closeness and mutual support. When you approach relationships with enthusiasm, you convey a sense of care and investment in the well-being of others, which can lead to deeper and more meaningful connections.

When the salesman 'senses' the fact that the 'psychological' moment for closing a sale has arrived, he merely feels the effect of his own enthusiasm as it influences the mind of his prospective buyer and places that mind 'en rapport' (in harmony) with his own. The subject of suggestion constitutes so vitally an important part of this lesson, and of this entire course, that I will now proceed to describe the three mediums through which it usually operates; namely, what you say, what you do, and what you think!

When you are enthusiastic over the goods you are selling or the services you are offering, or the speech you are delivering, your state of mind becomes obvious to all who hear you, by the tone of your voice. Whether you have ever thought of it in this way or not, it is the tone in which you make a statement, more than it is the statement itself, that carries conviction or fails to convince. No mere combination of words can ever take the place of a deep belief in a statement that is expressed with burning enthusiasm. Words are but devitalized sounds unless colored with feeling that is born of enthusiasm.

Here the printed word fails me, for I can never express with mere type and paper the difference between words that fall from unemotional lips, without the fire of enthusiasm back of them, and those which seem to pour forth from a heart that is bursting with eagerness for expression. The difference is there, however. Thus, what you say, and the way in which you say it, conveys a meaning that may be just the opposite to what is intended. This accounts for many a failure by the salesman who presents his arguments in words which seem logical enough, but lack the coloring that can come only from enthusiasm that is born of sincerity and belief in the goods he is trying to sell. His words said one thing, but the tone of his voice suggested something entirely different; therefore, no sale was made.

That which you say is an important factor in the operation of the principle of suggestion, but not nearly so important as that which you do. Your acts will count for more than your words, and woe unto you if the two fail to harmonize. When words and actions do not align, the resulting dissonance can create mistrust and skepticism in the minds of those you are trying to influence. Consistency between what you say and what you do is paramount to establishing credibility and trustworthiness.

The third medium through which suggestion operates is what you think. Your thoughts have a profound impact on your ability to influence others. When your mind is filled with positive, enthusiastic, and confident thoughts, this mental state becomes evident in your demeanor, expressions, and overall presence. Others can sense the energy and conviction emanating from you, even if they are not consciously aware of it. This subconscious perception can sway their opinions and decisions in your favor.

Conversely, if your thoughts are filled with doubt, fear, or negativity, these feelings will also manifest in your behavior and speech, often undermining your efforts to persuade or lead others. The power of thought, therefore, is a critical element in the principle of suggestion. By maintaining a mental attitude that is aligned with your goals and aspirations, you can project an image of certainty and enthusiasm that resonates with those around you.

If a salesman of Ford automobiles drives up to his prospective purchaser in a Buick or some other make of car, all the arguments he can present in behalf of the Ford will be without effect. Once I went into one of the offices of the Dictaphone Company to look at a Dictaphone (dictating machine). The salesman in charge presented a logical argument as to the machine's merits, while the stenographer at his side was transcribing letters from a shorthand notebook. His arguments in favor of a dictating machine, as compared with the old method of dictating to a stenographer, did not impress me because his actions were not in harmony with his words.

Your thoughts constitute the most important of the three ways in which you apply the principle of suggestion, for the reason that they control the tone of your words and, to some extent at least, your actions. If your thoughts and your actions and your words harmonize, you are bound to influence those with whom you come in contact, more or less toward your way of thinking.

We will now proceed to analyze the subject of suggestion and to show you exactly how to apply the principle upon which it operates. As we have already seen, suggestion differs from auto-suggestion only in one way—we use it, consciously or unconsciously, when we influence others, while we use Auto-suggestion as a means of influencing ourselves.

Before you can influence another person through suggestion, that person's mind must be in a state of neutrality; that is, it must be open and receptive to your method of suggestion. Right here is where most salesmen fail—they try to make a sale before the mind of the prospective buyer has been rendered receptive or neutralized. This is such a vital point in this lesson that I feel impelled to dwell upon it until there can be no doubt that you understand the principle that I am describing.

When I say that the salesman must neutralize the mind of his prospective purchaser before a sale can be made, I mean that the prospective purchaser's mind must be credulous. A state of confidence must have been established and it is obvious that there can be no set rule for either establishing confidence or neutralizing the mind to a state of openness. Here the ingenuity of the salesman must supply that which cannot be set down as a hard and fast rule.

I know a life insurance salesman who sells nothing but large policies, amounting to $100,000.00 and upward. Before this man even approaches the subject of insurance with a prospective client, he familiarizes himself with the prospective client's complete history, including his education, his financial status, his eccentricities if he has any, his religious preferences, and other data too numerous to be listed. Armed with this information, he manages to secure an introduction under conditions which permit him to know the prospective client in a social as well as a business way. Nothing is said about the sale of life insurance during his first visit, nor his second, and sometimes he does not approach the subject of insurance until he has become very well acquainted with the prospective client.

All this time, however, he is not dissipating his efforts. He is taking advantage of these friendly visits for the purpose of neutralizing his prospective client's mind; that is, he is building up a relationship of confidence so that when the time comes for him to talk life insurance, that which he says will fall upon ears that willingly listen.

Some years ago, I wrote a book entitled *How to Sell Your Services*. Just before the manuscript went to the publisher, it occurred to me to request some of the well-known men of the

United States to write letters of endorsement to be published in the book. The printer was then waiting for the manuscript; therefore, I hurriedly wrote a letter to some eight or ten men, in which I briefly outlined exactly what I wanted, but the letter brought back no replies. I had failed to observe two important prerequisites for success—I had written the letter so hurriedly that I had failed to inject the spirit of enthusiasm into it, and I had neglected to word the letter in a way that neutralized the minds of those to whom it was sent; therefore, I had not paved the way for the application of the principle of suggestion.

After I discovered my mistake, I then wrote a letter that was based upon the strict application of the principle of suggestion, and this letter not only brought back replies from all to whom it was sent, but many of the replies were masterpieces and served, far beyond my fondest hopes, as valuable supplements to the book.

NOT ALL ADVICE IS GOOD ADVICE

Suggestion is one of the most subtle and powerful principles of psychology. You are making use of it in all that you do, say, and think, but unless you understand the difference between negative suggestion and positive suggestion, you may be using it in a way that brings you defeat instead of success.

Science has established the fact that through the negative use of suggestion, life may be extinguished. Some years ago in France, a criminal was condemned to death. Before his execution, an experiment was performed on him which conclusively proved that through the principle of suggestion, death could be produced. The criminal was brought to the guillotine and his head was placed under the knife after he had been blindfolded.

A heavy, sharp-edged plank was then dropped on his neck, producing a shock similar to that of a sharp-edged knife. Warm water was then gently poured on his neck and allowed to trickle slowly down his spine to imitate the flow of warm blood. In seven minutes, the doctors pronounced the man dead. His imagination, through the principle of suggestion, had actually turned the sharp-edged plank into a guillotine blade and stopped his heart from beating.

In the little town where I was raised, there lived an old lady who constantly complained that she feared death from cancer. During her childhood, she had seen a woman with cancer, and the sight had so impressed itself upon her mind that she began to look for the symptoms of cancer in her own body. She was sure that every little ache and pain was the beginning of her long-looked-for symptom of cancer. I have seen her place her hand on her breast and heard her exclaim, 'Oh, I am sure I have a cancer growing here. I can feel it.' When complaining of this imaginary disease, she always placed her hand on her left breast, where she believed the cancer was attacking her.

For more than twenty years, she kept this up. A few weeks ago, she died—with cancer on her left breast! If suggestion can turn the edge of a plank into a guillotine blade and transform healthy body cells into parasites out of which cancer will develop, can you not imagine what it will do in destroying disease germs if properly directed? Suggestion is the law through which mental healers work what appear to be miracles. I have personally witnessed the removal of parasitical growths known as warts through the aid of suggestion within forty-eight hours.

You—the reader of this lesson—can be sent to bed with imaginary sickness of the worst sort in two hours' time or less through the use of suggestion. If you should start down the street and three or four people in whom you had confidence should meet you and each exclaim that you look ill, you would be ready for a doctor.

I wish to take advantage of this appropriate opportunity to state that all of the really big men whom I have had the pleasure of knowing have been the most willing and courteous men of my acquaintance when it came to rendering service that was of benefit to others. Perhaps that was one reason why they were really big men.

THE HUMAN MIND IS A MARVELOUS PIECE OF MACHINERY!

One of its outstanding characteristics is noticed in the fact that all impressions which reach it, either through outside suggestion or auto-suggestion, are recorded together in groups which harmonize in nature. The negative impressions are stored away, all in one portion of the brain, while the positive impressions are stored in another portion. When one of these impressions (or past experiences) is called into the conscious mind through the principle of memory, there is a tendency to recall with it all others of a similar nature, just as the raising of one link of a chain brings up other links with it.

For example, anything that causes a feeling of doubt to arise in a person's mind is sufficient to call forth all of his experiences which caused him to become doubtful. If a man is asked by a stranger to cash a check, immediately he remembers having cashed checks that were not good, or of having heard of others who did so. Through the law of association, all similar emotions, experiences, and sense impressions that reach the mind are filed away together, so that the recalling of one has a tendency to bring back to memory all the others.

The human mind's ability to categorize and recall impressions based on association is a fundamental aspect of cognition. By harnessing this understanding, individuals can navigate social interactions more effectively, whether in sales, personal relationships, or everyday communication. Recognizing and respecting the power of associative memory helps create environments conducive to constructive dialogue and positive outcomes.

This principle governs the entirety of human experience, influencing every impression stored in the mind. Consider fear: once a single fear-related emotion enters consciousness, it summons all associated negative feelings and memories. A feeling of courage cannot coexist while fear dominates; one inevitably overshadows the other. Their discordance illustrates that unlike emotions do not harmonize naturally; instead, like attracts like in the realm of conscious thought. Thus, each thought in the conscious mind tends to attract similar thoughts, forming interconnected networks of emotions and memories shaped by past experiences.

When using auto-suggestion, deliberately implanting ambitions or goals deep within the subconscious can awaken latent abilities and mobilize past experiences in one's favor. By consistently reinforcing a definite chief aim with enthusiasm, individuals can accelerate their progress towards their aspirations. Enthusiasm acts as the vitalizing force that ensures the suggestion's robust growth and enduring impact.

For example, instilling ambitions in a young person's mind—whether to become a lawyer, doctor, engineer, businessperson, or financier—through suggestion can profoundly influence their future path. By firmly embedding these ambitions and reinforcing them through repetition, one sets in motion a powerful psychological process that propels the individual towards realizing their goals.

To effectively embed suggestions deeply, enthusiasm is essential. It serves as the catalyst that ensures the suggestion takes root and flourishes in the subconscious. Enthusiasm not only facilitates rapid initial growth but also sustains the suggestion's potency over time, reinforcing its influence on thoughts, emotions, and actions. In essence, by understanding and harnessing the power of suggestion, individuals can unlock their potential and shape their reality. Whether for personal growth or influencing others positively, the deliberate and enthusiastic application of suggestion proves transformative, aligning thoughts and actions with desired outcomes. This approach underscores the profound impact of mindset and belief in shaping human potential and achievement.

When reflecting on the impact of the kind-hearted old gentleman's suggestion, it becomes clear that the manner and tone in which a message is delivered often leave a more profound imprint than the words themselves. His assurance that I was a 'bright boy' capable of making a significant mark in the world, coupled with the firm grip on my shoulders and the confidence gleaming in his eyes, embedded the suggestion deep within my subconscious. This combination of words, touch, and demeanor worked in unison to ignite a relentless drive within me to pursue education and achieve my aspirations.

This anecdote underscores a critical point: the effectiveness of communication is heavily influenced by the emotional content and sincerity behind it. It's not merely the words spoken, but the tone and manner in which they are conveyed that create lasting impressions. The genuine belief and earnestness behind the message amplify its impact, resonating deeply within the recipient's subconscious mind and motivating action.

Therefore, sincerity of purpose, honesty, and earnestness are essential attributes that should underpin every message delivered. When these qualities are authentically present, they enhance credibility and trust, ensuring that the message is received positively and with lasting effect. People are naturally attuned to sincerity and respond more favorably when they sense genuine intent and integrity in the speaker. The principle extends beyond personal interactions to professional endeavors. In sales or persuasion, for instance, convincing others of a product's value or a concept's merit requires first convincing oneself. Belief in the message's worthiness and benefits is essential to conveying it convincingly and persuasively to others. This alignment between personal conviction and external communication reinforces the message's authenticity and persuasiveness.

In conclusion, by prioritizing sincerity, honesty, and earnestness in our interactions, we not only make lasting impressions but also foster trust and credibility. Whether inspiring personal growth or achieving professional success, the way we communicate and believe in our messages shapes our ability to influence and motivate others positively.

5

Sunshine in Your Pocket

A life enriched with wealth and profound inner peace often finds its foundation in the cultivation and steadfast maintenance of a positive mental attitude. This mindset, when coupled with a resolute definiteness of purpose, imbues individuals with the necessary positive energy to propel them towards their goals. It allows them not only to set clear objectives but also to sustain their efforts with unwavering determination. Moreover, by establishing spiritual guardians—symbolic entities that safeguard positivity and ward off conflicting motivations—one can fortify their mental resilience and attract beneficial influences from like-minded individuals in their journey towards success and fulfillment.

Consider the analogy of computers, which play an increasingly pivotal role in managing our modern world. Despite their intricacies, these machines operate on a fundamentally binary principle of Yes or No. Similarly, within the human mind, there exists a critical Yes-No valve that determines our response to life's stimuli. Everything perceived by our senses undergoes processing through this valve, where individuals with a positive outlook tend to lean towards affirmation—seizing opportunities, acknowledging the silver linings in challenges, and integrating positive outcomes into their lives. Conversely, those shackled by a negative mindset often gravitate towards the negative pole, missing out on opportunities, fixating on the painful aspects of life, and inadvertently fostering a cycle of discontent.

It might seem overly simplistic to attribute profound life outcomes solely to mental attitude. However, the truth lies in the profound impact it wields over our lives, influencing our peace of mind versus chronic anxiety, our predisposition towards robust health versus susceptibility to illness. The transformative power of adopting a positive mental attitude cannot be overstated; it enables individuals to reframe challenges as opportunities for growth, to approach setbacks with resilience, and to sustain optimism even amidst adversity.

The journey from negativism to positivism is not only possible but essential for anyone seeking to harness the full spectrum of life's richness. Moreover, the Creator has endowed us with various 'control levers'—fundamental principles and actionable insights that, when applied diligently, empower individuals to shape their destinies. Throughout this book, I will expound upon these levers, reinforcing your understanding through repetition of key concepts, names, and methodologies. This deliberate reinforcement aims to embed these transformative principles deep within your psyche, equipping you with the wisdom and tools necessary to elevate your mental attitude and manifest a life abundant in wealth, peace, and fulfillment.

Controlling your mental attitude through definiteness of purpose is akin to wielding a powerful tool for navigating life's complexities with clarity and resilience. Ralph Waldo Emerson's assertion, 'The world makes way for a man who knows where he is going,' encapsulates the transformative impact of having a clear direction in life. When you possess a definite purpose, you automatically dispel uncertainties and anxieties that might otherwise cloud your decision-making process. Your mind becomes a magnet for focus and determination, harnessing its boundless energies to pursue that singular purpose with unwavering commitment.

Consider the practical implications: where once your endeavors may have been scattered or diluted by indecision or distraction, now every mental and physical effort converges towards achieving your chosen goal. This alignment not only enhances your productivity but also amplifies your effectiveness in wealth-building endeavors. By executing tasks with precision and dedication, you optimize your potential to generate prosperity and success.

Moreover, the connection between definiteness of purpose and peace of mind becomes evident. A person fully engaged in pursuing their purpose is less prone to distractions such as fault-finding or compromising their integrity in their work. They are not consumed by trivial concerns like watching the clock or fretting over obstacles; instead, their positive and focused mental attitude equips them to confront challenges head-on and overcome them with resilience and resourcefulness.

Cultivating a clear purpose in life acts as a guiding beacon, steering you away from the pitfalls of indecision and doubt. It empowers you to harness your mental faculties and channel them towards constructive actions that lead to both material wealth and inner peace. By maintaining this disciplined approach, you fortify your capacity to navigate life's complexities with confidence, ensuring that each endeavor contributes meaningfully to your overall success and well-being.

CULTIVATING POSITIVITY

Efficiency and positivity stand as defining traits often associated with genius. This correlation is evident in the lives of remarkable individuals such as Henry Ford, Andrew Carnegie, and Thomas A. Edison. Despite not possessing exceptional intelligence beyond their contemporaries, these figures achieved feats that elevated them to the status of geniuses. What set them apart was not innate brilliance but their unwavering positive mental attitude, which allowed them to leverage their existing abilities with unparalleled efficiency and effectiveness.

Andrew Carnegie, a shrewd Scot known for his business acumen, understood keenly the pivotal role of a positive mental attitude in achieving success. When presented with an opportunity that would alter the course of his life, the author faced a critical juncture. Andrew Carnegie, well-aware of the importance of mindset, posed a straightforward yet profound question. He laid out the terms clearly, asking whether the author was willing to commit two decades to a venture that promised fame, wealth, and influence. It was a challenge that demanded not just skill or intellect, but unwavering resolve and a positive outlook.

In that crucial moment, doubts and uncertainties briefly clouded the author's mind. The enormity of the task ahead, the uncertainties of financial stability, and the long road of dedication required all loomed large. For twenty-nine seconds, the author grappled internally with a negative mental attitude that threatened to undermine the opportunity before him.

However, in a flash of insight and determination, the tide turned. The author reclaimed clarity and decisively responded with a resounding 'Yes!' This pivotal decision, though seemingly brief, marked a definitive turning point. It was a testament not only to the author's courage and commitment but also to the transformative power of maintaining a positive mental attitude.

Andrew Carnegie's gesture of revealing a stopwatch underscored the significance of that moment. The author's response, beating the deadline by a mere thirty-one seconds, symbolized more than a mere agreement—it signified a profound alignment of mindset and opportunity. This alignment would go on to shape not only the author's personal destiny but also influence the lives of countless others worldwide.

This anecdote serves as a poignant reminder that genius is often less about innate intelligence and more about the resilience and positivity that individuals bring to their endeavors. It highlights the critical importance of maintaining a positive mental attitude in navigating challenges, seizing opportunities, and achieving remarkable feats. Andrew Carnegie's test of mental attitude remains a timeless lesson in fortitude and vision—showcasing how, amidst uncertainties and adversity, a positive outlook can serve as a guiding light towards personal fulfillment and significant societal impact.

A positive mental attitude not only empowers an individual internally but also aligns them with external sources of positivity and success. Once I committed to the daunting task presented by Andrew Carnegie and focused my mind resolutely on it, I noticed that perceived obstacles dissolved effortlessly. My positive mindset not only facilitated my discovery of the success principles from over five hundred of America's wealthiest individuals but also enabled me to achieve far more than mere survival. Am I a genius? I possess conclusive evidence to the contrary!

Through my interactions with numerous successful men, including luminaries like John Wanamaker, Frank A. Vanderlip, Edward Bok, and Woodrow Wilson, I uncovered a profound truth: a positive mind naturally attracts benefits from other positive minds. Consider the principle of radio broadcasting—an electrical signal sent through a wire can be picked up by a distant receiving antenna, transmitting messages or images across vast distances. Similarly, the electrical currents in our brains serve as a private broadcasting station, allowing us to transmit thought vibrations of our choosing.

By keeping this mental station busy with positive thoughts that benefit others, we tune ourselves into a frequency that attracts similar vibrations from like-minded individuals. When I engaged with successful men of stature, seeking their time and wisdom, there was a palpable alignment of minds. Far from encountering resistance, these leaders generously shared their insights and mentored me for years without expecting anything in return.

Believing wholeheartedly in your endeavors has a profound impact on those you approach for assistance. Confidence in yourself sends a signal of assurance, inviting cooperation and support. Conversely, harboring doubts allows negativity to take hold, sabotaging potential success and drawing defeat rather than victory.

The influence of a positive mental attitude extends far beyond individual empowerment—it acts as a catalyst when combined with other 'control levers' that shape a life of wealth and peace. This brief overview merely scratches the surface of its pervasive power. In the chapters ahead, we will delve into these levers and explore how they, in concert with a positive mindset, pave the way for a lifetime of triumph and fulfillment.

THE NINE MAJOR MOTIVES

It is not without reason that court trials often revolve around questions of motive. Motive is the driving force behind every action we take, every decision we make. Our actions are influenced by one or more of these fundamental motives, which can be categorized into seven positive and two negative emotions.

The Seven Positive Motives

1. **The Emotion of Love:** Love is a powerful motivator. It can inspire acts of kindness, generosity, and selflessness. Love for family, friends, and even humanity at large can drive individuals to achieve great things and to make sacrifices for the benefit of others.
2. **The Emotion of Sex:** This primal urge is not only about physical gratification but also encompasses a broader desire for intimacy, connection, and partnership. It is a powerful force that can lead to creative and life-affirming actions.
3. **The Desire for Material Gain:** The pursuit of wealth and material success motivates many to work hard, innovate, and strive for financial stability and prosperity. This desire can lead to economic progress and the betterment of living conditions.
4. **The Desire for Self-Preservation:** The instinct to protect oneself from harm, whether physical or emotional, drives many of our actions. This fundamental motive ensures that we take steps to secure our well-being and survival.
5. **The Desire for Freedom of Body and Mind:** The yearning for liberty, whether from physical constraints or mental oppression, propels individuals to fight for rights, pursue education, and seek personal and societal liberation.
6. **The Desire for Self-Expression:** The need to express oneself, to share one's ideas, talents, and emotions, fuels creativity and innovation. This motive drives artists, writers, thinkers, and creators of all kinds to contribute to the cultural and intellectual wealth of society.

7. **The Desire for Perpetuation of Life After Death:** Many seek to leave a lasting legacy, to be remembered and honored long after they are gone. This desire motivates people to engage in activities that will have a lasting impact, such as philanthropy, mentoring, and creating enduring works.

The Two Negative Motives

1. **The Emotion of Anger and Revenge:** Anger, when uncontrolled, can lead to a desire for revenge and harmful actions. It is a destructive force that can ruin relationships, disrupt peace, and cause significant harm to oneself and others.
2. **The Emotion of Fear:** Fear is a paralyzing emotion that can prevent individuals from taking action, pursuing goals, and realizing their potential. It can stem from various sources, such as fear of failure, rejection, or the unknown.

The Impact of Motives on Peace of Mind

Peace of mind is achievable when one's life is primarily governed by the seven positive motives. These motives foster a sense of fulfillment, purpose, and harmony. On the other hand, individuals who consistently act out of anger or fear are unlikely to find peace of mind. These negative emotions disrupt mental tranquility, lead to destructive behaviors, and prevent the cultivation of a positive and serene outlook on life.

A person who lives in fear cannot experience true peace. Fear breeds anxiety, stress, and insecurity, making it impossible to relax and enjoy life. Similarly, harboring anger and seeking revenge creates a cycle of negativity that consumes one's thoughts and actions. This preoccupation with negative emotions prevents the development of a balanced and peaceful state of mind.

In conclusion, understanding and harnessing the nine major motives can lead to a more deliberate and fulfilling life. By focusing on the positive motives and minimizing the influence of negative emotions, one can achieve not only external success but also internal peace. It is a matter of aligning one's actions with motives that promote growth, well-being, and harmony, thereby fostering a life of richness and contentment.

THE PRICE OF PEACE OF MIND

Great men do not waste their time harboring desires to harm others. If they did, they would not be considered great. While great men are not immune to fear, they do not let fear dominate their lives. Instead, they manage it, preventing it from overshadowing their goals and aspirations. In contrast, small, mean men often exhibit lifelong patterns of fear and anger. Their minds are so consumed by these negative emotions that they lack the ability to shape their circumstances positively.

Consider the story of a man, now seventy years old, who fifteen years ago lost all his money in a real estate venture. Following a friend's advice, he borrowed heavily to invest in vacant swampland, believing it would soon be in high demand for building lots. Unfortunately, this did not happen. The man's debts came due, and he was forced to sell his retail shoe business to cover the losses. Despite his friend also losing money in the deal, the man became filled with hatred and vowed to get even, saying, 'if it's the last thing I do.'

This vengeful mindset consumed him for five years, rendering him incapable of conducting any business. Meanwhile, his friend prospered, seemingly untouchable by any attempt at revenge. The man who had lost his money eventually lost his mental stability and had to spend six months in a secluded place surrounded by a high wall. During his last month of confinement, he recovered enough to listen to an adviser who pointed out that his hatred and desire for revenge had caused him far more harm than the financial loss. Persuaded to forgive his friend, he wrote a letter expressing his change of heart.

Returning to business with a renewed spirit, he focused on love for his fellow men and filled his mind with positive, constructive motives. Starting anew at sixty, he rebuilt his career. Now, at seventy, he is relatively well-off and, most importantly, has achieved peace of mind—the one form of wealth that is truly indispensable.

I, too, have experienced the effects of negative motives. During a period of hiding, I initially acted out of self-preservation. However, this soon turned into fear, bringing misery along with it. Fortunately, I recognized what was happening in time, ensuring it will not happen again.

The Ten Princes of Guidance

In safeguarding your mind, it is crucial to establish protective measures that ensure only beneficial thoughts and influences enter your consciousness. To achieve this, I have conceptualized ten guiding principles, personified as Princes, each responsible for maintaining a specific aspect of your mental well-being. Here is an expanded explanation of these ten guiding principles:

1. *The Prince of Peace of Mind*

The Prince of Peace of Mind stands vigilant at the very outer door of your consciousness. His role is to scrutinize every thought and influence that attempts to enter. He asks each one if they come in peace to share in and contribute to your tranquility. If the answer is no, they are turned away, ensuring that your peace of mind remains unperturbed. This Prince is essential for maintaining an environment free from conflict and turmoil, allowing you to think clearly and act calmly.

2. *The Prince of Hope and Faith*

The Prince of Hope and Faith is dedicated to keeping your mind infused with belief in your life's mission. He admits only those influences that bolster your confidence and sustain your dreams and aspirations. By ensuring that hope and faith are ever-present in your thoughts, this Prince helps you overcome doubts and stay motivated, regardless of the challenges you face.

3. *The Prince of Love and Romance*

The Prince of Love and Romance ensures that only influences that keep love eternally fresh in your heart are allowed in. This Prince nurtures your capacity for love, fostering deep connections and maintaining the emotional warmth that enriches your relationships. By keeping your heart open and loving, this Prince helps you build and sustain meaningful bonds with others.

4. *The Prince of Sound Physical Health*

The Prince of Sound Physical Health is tasked with safeguarding your physical well-being by allowing only those mental influences that contribute to your body's vigor. He recognizes the detrimental effects of negative thoughts on your health and diligently keeps them at bay. By promoting a healthy mindbody connection, this Prince ensures that your physical health supports your overall success and happiness.

5. *The Prince of Financial Security*

The Prince of Financial Security stands guard over your financial well-being. He admits only those thoughts and influences that bring worthy financial benefit. This Prince helps you cultivate a mindset of abundance and prudent financial management, ensuring that your efforts lead to lasting economic stability and prosperity.

6. *The Prince of Overall Wisdom*

The Prince of Overall Wisdom is responsible for discerning which thoughts should be added to your store of knowledge. He admits only those ideas and insights that will benefit you or help you benefit others. By fostering a continuous pursuit of learning and understanding, this Prince ensures that your decisions are informed and wise, contributing to your long-term success and growth.

7. *The Prince of Patience*

The Prince of Patience is essential for maintaining a measured and thoughtful approach to life. He keeps away all impulses to rush, tackle jobs half-prepared, or be impatient with the natural pace of time. By fostering patience, this Prince helps you approach tasks methodically, ensuring thorough preparation and execution. This patience prevents hasty decisions and allows for a more thoughtful and deliberate path to success.

8. The Prince of Persistence

The Prince of Persistence stands as a constant reminder to never give up. He ensures that the drive to continue pushing forward, regardless of obstacles, remains strong. This Prince helps you develop the tenacity to stay the course, even when challenges seem insurmountable. By cultivating a persistent mindset, you increase your chances of achieving long-term goals and realizing your fullest potential.

9. The Prince of Creativity

The Prince of Creativity is dedicated to keeping your imagination active and vibrant. He admits thoughts and influences that inspire innovative thinking and creative problem-solving. By fostering a creative mindset, this Prince helps you find unique solutions to challenges and approach opportunities with a fresh perspective. Creativity is a key driver of progress and can set you apart in your endeavors.

10. The Prince of Integrity

The Prince of Integrity ensures that your actions align with your core values and principles. He admits only those thoughts that promote honesty, trustworthiness, and ethical behavior. By maintaining a strong sense of integrity, this Prince helps you build a reputation of reliability and respect, which is crucial for lasting success and meaningful relationships.

These Princes, or guiding principles, will help you maintain a positive mental attitude, free of the negative emotions that can lead to failure and misery. By actively cultivating these positive motives and avoiding the negative ones, you can achieve not only external success but also internal peace and fulfillment.

The Prince of Normhill

The Prince of Normhill is a uniquely personal guardian, a concept tailored specifically to my own needs and experiences. 'Normhill' is a word I created by combining certain names that hold significant meaning for me. It represents a unique entity that resonates with my personal journey, something no one else can fully understand or replicate. Just as I have created this name for my personal guardian, I encourage you to create a name for your own special Prince. This guardian stands alongside the other Princes, vigilantly protecting and guiding you. While other Princes may take turns in their duties—for example, it may not be necessary to constantly focus on financial security—your personal Prince remains ever-present, embodying all the unique personal influences in your life. Normhill serves as my ambassador-at-large, handling tasks and challenges not specifically assigned to the other members of my invisible family of guides.

When you become deeply familiar with your spiritual Princes, they can collectively rally to address any problem or establish special defenses as needed. For instance, there are moments when I find myself in conversation with someone whose antagonistic attitude threatens my peace of mind. In such cases, I send a special alert to the Prince of Peace of Mind. Instantly, he fortifies my mental defenses with renewed vigor, allowing me to remain calm and in control of my thoughts and emotions.

Similarly, if I experience a physical ache or discomfort, I call upon the Prince of Sound Physical Health to investigate and address the cause. This proactive approach often yields remarkable results, and I believe I have experienced benefits that transcend the explanations of conventional medical science. My faith in this Prince's ability to heal and maintain my physical well-being has brought me comfort and relief in ways that are both profound and unexplainable by ordinary means.

In essence, the Prince of Normhill and the other Princes form a comprehensive support system that ensures my mental, emotional, and physical well-being. By recognizing and nurturing these guardians, you too can harness their power to maintain a balanced and fulfilled life. These spiritual Princes work tirelessly to safeguard your peace of mind, health, and overall prosperity, ensuring that you remain resilient and focused on your path to success.

Compensation for My Princes of Guidance

My Princes of Guidance receive a unique form of compensation for their unwavering service: my eternal gratitude. Each day, I take the time to express this gratitude, individually acknowledging each Prince and then honoring them as a formidable collective. This daily practice of gratitude helps keep my mind attuned to its own powers and the spiritual forces at my disposal. I have noticed that if I ever neglect this practice, it feels as though my Princes become less active in my life. However, once I resume my daily expressions of gratitude, they return with renewed vigor, as strong and supportive as ever.

Balancing Material Gain and Freedom

It's crucial not to let the motive of material gain conflict with the equally important motive of freedom. Freedom of body is straightforward and easy to understand; it encompasses physical liberty and the ability to move and act without restraint. However, freedom of mind is a subtler and more intricate matter. Negative emotions such as fear and anger can imprison the mind, while guilt can wrap it in unbreakable chains.

To illustrate the seriousness of mental freedom with a touch of humor, consider the story of a man who was encouraged to know himself better. Taking this advice quite literally, he handcuffed himself to his bed to prevent himself from getting up and rifling through his own pockets during the night. This amusing anecdote underscores how inner conflicts and unresolved issues can severely restrict our mental freedom.

All too often, the desire for material gain—valuable and motivating as it is—clashes with the motive of maintaining freedom of mind and body. This conflict arises when we pursue material wealth dishonestly, burdening our minds with guilt and fear due to our unethical actions. Furthermore, those who acquire wealth through deceit and exploitation of others deprive themselves of the profound satisfaction and genuine joy that accompany honest success. Winning through fair play nourishes the soul and builds character, while cheating may yield material rewards but ultimately leaves one spiritually impoverished.

Early Life Lessons and Their Impact

Reflecting on my journey, I feel fortunate to have embarked on my career at an early age, which allowed me to learn life's important lessons sooner than many. My first job, just after graduating from business college, provided a rich ground for these lessons. At that time, I was inexperienced in the ways of the world and the complexities of human character. This early exposure to the realities of business and interpersonal relations was instrumental in shaping my understanding and approach to success.

In one of my earliest professional experiences, I encountered situations that tested my integrity and decision-making. These formative moments taught me the value of honesty, the importance of maintaining a positive mental attitude, and the necessity of balancing different motives in life. By learning these lessons early, I was better prepared to navigate the challenges of my career and personal growth, building a foundation for lasting success and peace of mind.

Gratitude and the Power of Positive Influence

The practice of daily gratitude towards my Princes of Guidance is more than a ritual; it is a powerful tool for maintaining a positive and focused mindset. Each Prince plays a vital role in my mental and spiritual well-being, ensuring that I remain resilient and capable in the face of life's challenges. By actively expressing gratitude, I reinforce my awareness of these spiritual guardians and their influence, which in turn strengthens their ability to support and guide me.

This reciprocal relationship between gratitude and spiritual guidance highlights the importance of maintaining a positive mental attitude and being mindful of the influences we allow into our lives. By consciously choosing to focus on positive thoughts and actions, we attract similar positive energies and create a virtuous cycle of growth, success, and inner peace.

In conclusion, the balance between material gain and freedom, the lessons learned from early life experiences, and the daily practice of gratitude towards my spiritual Princes are all integral to my philosophy of success. These elements work together to ensure that I remain grounded, focused, and aligned with my higher purpose, enabling me to achieve not only material wealth but also the invaluable wealth of peace of mind.

My employer was a prominent figure in the financial industry, owning a number of banks. His son held a position as a cashier at one of these banks, situated in a distant town. One night, I received an urgent phone call from a hotel manager in that town. The manager informed me that my employer's son was in serious trouble, and despite numerous attempts, he had been unable to reach my employer. Without hesitation, I boarded a train and arrived in the town early the following morning.

Upon my arrival at the bank, I found the door closed but unlocked. Inside, the scene was startling: the vault was wide open, and beautiful green currency was scattered across the teller's counter. Realizing the gravity of the situation, I immediately closed the door and picked up the telephone to call my employer. I explained why I had come to the town and described the scene that greeted me upon my arrival. My employer, distressed, instructed me, 'Go ahead and count the money. Balance the books. Draw a draft on me for whatever shortage there may be.'

I began the meticulous task of counting the money. To my immense surprise, every cent was accounted for; not a single dollar was missing. As I sat there, looking at those piles of greenbacks, I couldn't help but reflect on my past. My youth had been filled with tragedy, turbulence, and poverty. At that moment, my financial situation was barely solvent. Here I was, surrounded by nearly $50,000 in cash, knowing that I could easily pocket at least half of it, and no one would be the wiser. My employer's son exhibited clear signs of mental instability, and it would be all too easy for everyone to assume he had taken the money. He had even behaved in a manner that suggested he had filled his own pockets—and I was the only one who knew he had not.

The motive of material gain tugged heavily at me. The idea of securing a significant sum of money was tempting. However, another powerful force, the motive of freedom, whispered to me, 'Don't do it.' At that time, I might not have been able to articulate the major motives, but there was 'something' that kept me honest. Perhaps it was the result of the sessions I had had with my stepmother before leaving home, sessions in which she instilled in me the importance of being in control of my own mind and always living with integrity.

I locked the money back into the vault and phoned my employer once more. I informed him that there was no deficiency to make up; not a single cent had been stolen. As I walked out of that bank, I felt an overwhelming sense of peace and freedom. My mind was joyous and positively charged.

From that day forward, I vowed to always place the motive of freedom ahead of the motive of material gain. This principle has guided me throughout my life, allowing me to achieve all the financial success I need without ever compromising my inward or outward freedom. The peace of mind that comes from knowing I have acted with integrity is invaluable, and it has been a cornerstone of my personal and professional life. This experience reinforced my belief in the power of maintaining a positive mental attitude and the importance of ethical behavior in all circumstances.

Life is a Mirror

This episode was one of several pivotal moments that led me directly to Andrew Carnegie and the realization of my life's purpose. My employer, grateful for my integrity in protecting his son's reputation, later facilitated my entry into Georgetown University Law School. This chain of events eventually led to my assignment to interview Mr. Carnegie. Had I yielded to the temptation of material gain that day in the bank, the Science of Personal Achievement might never have come into being.

As Emerson suggested, there is a silent partner in all our transactions, and woe to the man who tries to drive a sharp bargain with Life. Life reflects your own thoughts back to you. A poet once said, 'Thoughts are things,' and indeed, they possess an existence of their own. A curse comes back to curse you, and a blessing returns to bless you, reflected by the mighty mirror of life. Another poet declared, 'I am the master of my fate, I am the captain of my soul.' This, too, is true, and these two truths harmonize. Send out positive thoughts from a positively oriented soul, and the world will reflect back greater and greater positive influences to support you.

The Nine Basic Motives

Let's revisit the nine basic motives. Concentrate on the seven positive motives. While these motives can occasionally come into conflict, they generally drive in one direction, and with a positive mental attitude, they lead you where you want to go. We won't say farewell to the motives until we finish this book, but let us briefly pay our respects to them now.

1. **Love**: Love has limitless scope. Handle it with reverence, for it is tuned to the Eternal. Give love freely, and you will attract as much, if not more, than you give. Stop giving love, and you stop receiving. The mirror of life reflects no other emotion or motive as clearly as it does love.
2. **Sex**: Sex is the great creative force of the universe. On its highest plane, it merges with love, though love can exist without being sexual. The mighty power of sex can be

transmuted into action for the achievement of profound purposes. Later, we shall devote an entire chapter to this subject. Conversely, sex can be debased and misused, bringing grief and trouble to mankind and giving itself an undeserved bad reputation.

3. **Self-preservation**: This motive can become a negative force when sought without regard for the rights of others. Instilled by Nature to help us stay alive, it can be transcended by human nobility. For example, in a sinking ship, it is women and children first. Many parallel instances call forth this nobility in human nature.

4. **Material Gain**: The desire for material gain is a powerful motivator. However, it must be pursued ethically, without compromising one's freedom of mind or body. True wealth includes not just financial prosperity but also peace of mind and integrity.

5. **Freedom of Body and Mind**: Freedom of body is easy to understand, but freedom of mind is more subtle. Fear and anger imprison the mind, while guilt wraps it in chains. True freedom involves acting honestly and without deceit, thereby keeping the mind unencumbered by negative emotions.

6. **Self-expression**: This motive drives individuals to share their unique talents and ideas with the world. It is through self-expression that one can leave a lasting impact and achieve personal fulfillment.

7. **Perpetuation of Life After Death**: This motive encompasses the desire to leave a legacy, to ensure that one's influence and contributions continue beyond one's lifetime. It can inspire actions that benefit future generations and contribute to the greater good.

8. **Anger and Revenge**: These negative emotions can destroy peace of mind and lead to destructive behaviors. Harboring

anger and seeking revenge ultimately harms the individual more than the target of their wrath.
9. **Fear**: Fear is a paralyzing force that prevents individuals from taking risks and seizing opportunities. Overcoming fear is essential for personal growth and achievement.

Integrating the Motives

These motives, when properly understood and harnessed, can drive you towards success and fulfillment. However, it is crucial to maintain a balance and prioritize the positive motives over the negative ones. By doing so, you can ensure that your actions are aligned with your values and contribute to your overall well-being.

Reflecting on my own journey, I realize that the alignment of my motives and maintaining a positive mental attitude were key to achieving my goals. The silent partner in all our transactions—life itself—responds to the thoughts and attitudes we project. By consistently sending out positive thoughts and aligning our actions with positive motives, we can shape our reality and achieve true success and peace of mind.

Self-Expression and Perpetuation of Life

Self-expression is an essential part of discovering and understanding oneself. It is integral to one's freedom to be authentic, making it a positive, constructive, and infinitely valuable pursuit. However, it is crucial to ensure that your means of self-expression do not demean or harm others. True self-expression uplifts both the individual and those around them. It allows one to communicate their innermost thoughts, feelings, and creativity, fostering a sense of fulfillment and personal growth. This process of expressing oneself can take many forms, such as art, writing, speaking, or any other medium that resonates with the individual's soul. By embracing self-expression, you not only enrich your own life but also contribute to the diversity and richness of the human experience.

Perpetuation of life after death is among humanity's oldest beliefs and motivations. It should be guided by common sense and a true understanding of our relationship with the concept of death. When this motive is wrapped in superstition and fear, it leads to misery and can turn life into a mere preparation for death, potentially hampering entire civilizations. Instead, a balanced and rational approach to this motive can bring comfort and purpose, enriching life rather than detracting from it. Believing in an afterlife or in leaving a legacy can inspire people to live more meaningfully and ethically, knowing that their actions have lasting impacts. This perspective encourages individuals to contribute positively to the world, creating a ripple effect that benefits future generations.

The Surest Way to Peace of Mind

The surest way to achieve peace of mind is to help the greatest number of others find it. This principle should guide your use of the great motivating forces. When you ensure your actions are beneficial to others, you can be confident that you are using these forces correctly, without corruption. Helping others find peace of mind involves acts of kindness, empathy, and support. By being a source of comfort and stability for those around you, you create an environment where peace can flourish. This, in turn, reflects back on you, reinforcing your own sense of inner peace. Engaging in community service, supporting loved ones, and promoting a culture of understanding and respect are ways to extend peace of mind to others, ultimately enriching your own life.

The Role of Prayer in Achieving Peace of Mind

Is there peace of mind in prayer? There can and should be. However, many people resort to prayer only in times of misfortune, driven by fear. This negative approach often leads to negative results in terms of peace of mind. Effective prayers, those that bring peace and solve problems, come from a mind that exudes confidence despite facing challenges. These prayers are born from the belief that problems can be solved once the necessary forces are found, with unwavering confidence in the existence of these forces. Prayer, when practiced with a positive mindset, can be a powerful tool for aligning one's intentions with the greater good. It can provide solace, clarity, and a sense of connection to a higher power or the universe. Regular prayer or meditation fosters a sense of calm and resilience, enabling individuals to navigate life's challenges with grace and strength.

Many, including myself, see evidence of an Intelligence beyond human comprehension. A positively conditioned mind may occasionally tune into this Intelligence. Yet, conditioning the mind through prayer or resolution is a personal endeavor. When the Creator endowed humanity with the freedom to seek its own destiny and choose between good and evil, this prerogative was included. Every great accomplishment of any person had to exist first as a thought before it could become reality. This process of visualization and intention-setting is fundamental to achieving one's goals. By focusing your thoughts and prayers on positive outcomes and aligning your actions with these intentions, you create a pathway for success. Believing in a higher intelligence or a guiding force can enhance your sense of purpose and provide the strength needed to overcome obstacles.

The Supreme Secret

Have you recognized the Supreme Secret? The essence of this secret lies in understanding that life reflects your own thoughts back to you. A poet once said, 'Thoughts are things,' implying that they possess an existence of their own. A curse returns to curse you, and a blessing returns to bless you, mirrored by the vast expanse of life. Another poet stated, 'I am the master of my fate, I am the captain of my soul,' emphasizing personal responsibility and control over one's destiny. These truths harmonize beautifully: positive thoughts from a positively oriented soul attract greater positive influences from the world.

Reflecting on the list of nine basic motives, particularly the seven positive ones, can help you align your actions with your goals. Although these motives can occasionally conflict, they generally drive you in a unified direction. By maintaining a positive mental attitude, you can harness these motives to take you where you want to go. Embracing these motives involves continuous self-reflection and adjustment. By regularly evaluating your thoughts and actions, you ensure that they remain aligned with your core values and goals. This ongoing process of self-improvement and positive reinforcement creates a cycle of success and fulfillment, reinforcing the Supreme Secret's power.

Embracing Love, Sex, and Self-Preservation

Love has limitless scope and should be handled with reverence, as it is connected to the Eternal. Give love freely, and you will receive it in abundance. Cease to give love, and you will cease to receive it. Life's mirror is most evident with love. Love enriches your life by fostering deep connections and a sense of belonging. It can manifest in various forms, such as romantic love, familial love, and platonic love, each contributing to your overall well-being. By nurturing love in all its forms, you create a network of support and positivity that enhances your life's quality.

Sex, the great creative force of the universe, can merge with love on its highest plane, though love can exist without being sexual. The power of sex can be transmuted into actions that achieve profound purposes. Misused, it brings grief and trouble, tarnishing its reputation. Understanding and respecting the power of sex involves recognizing its potential for both creation and destruction. When harnessed positively, it can inspire creativity, intimacy, and profound connections. Educating oneself about healthy sexual expression and relationships ensures that this potent force is used to enhance life rather than detract from it.

Self-preservation is a natural instinct, helping us stay alive. However, it can become negative when pursued without regard for others' rights. The human spirit has the capacity to transcend self-preservation. In critical situations, such as a sinking ship, the nobility of 'women and children first' exemplifies this transcendence. Self-preservation should be balanced with empathy and altruism. By recognizing our shared humanity and acting with compassion, we can rise above purely self-serving instincts. This balance fosters a sense of community and mutual support, ensuring that the drive for self-preservation does not compromise ethical principles or the well-being of others.

By focusing on positive motives like love, self-expression, and self-preservation balanced with a higher purpose, you can achieve success and peace of mind. Ensure that your actions align with these motives and contribute to your overall well-being. Remember, life reflects your thoughts and actions, and by maintaining a positive mental attitude, you can create a life filled with success, fulfillment, and peace. Aligning your motives involves setting clear goals and intentions, regularly assessing your progress, and making necessary adjustments. This proactive approach ensures that your actions remain in harmony with your values and aspirations, leading to sustained success and inner peace.

6

Unleashing Collective Brilliance

If you had a definite major purpose, knew exactly what you wanted to achieve, had a mastermind alliance of people who could assist you in accomplishing it, and possessed the unwavering faith to keep you moving forward, that would encompass almost everything you need to succeed. These elements—clear purpose, a supportive network, and steadfast faith—are fundamental to any significant achievement.

But why, then, do we need the additional fourteen principles? The reason is that these three core elements alone are not sufficient in isolation. We need the additional principles to guide and amplify the use of these foundational aspects. The extra principles provide the necessary framework and tools to ensure the effective application and realization of your purpose.

Consider the importance of personal initiative. This principle drives you to take the necessary steps towards your goals without external prompting. It's about being proactive and taking charge of your own progress. Without personal initiative, even the most well-laid plans can falter due to inaction.

Imagination is another crucial principle. It allows you to

visualize your goals and devise creative solutions to obstacles that may arise. Imagination fuels innovation and keeps your approach dynamic and adaptable. Enthusiasm, meanwhile, is the energy and passion that propels you forward. It's the spark that keeps you motivated and engaged, even in the face of challenges.

This philosophy can be likened to baking a cake. When baking, you don't rely on just one ingredient. Instead, you combine a variety of ingredients—a pinch of this, a dash of that, and a smidge of something else. Each ingredient plays a critical role in creating the final product. Omit any one of these ingredients, and the result would not be the same. Similarly, this philosophy relies on a harmonious blend of principles. Neglecting even one of these seventeen principles would be like removing a link from a chain. You'd end up with a fragmented chain, unable to function as a whole.

The fourteen additional principles serve as the supporting framework for the three foundational ones. They fill in the gaps, providing the necessary structure and direction to ensure your efforts are comprehensive and effective.

Faith, in this context, is more than just a passive state of mind; it's been described as the mainspring of the soul. It's the driving force that transforms your aims, desires, plans, and purposes into their physical or financial equivalent. While the fundamentals of faith are essential, applied faith goes beyond mere belief. The term 'applied' signifies action. It's the practical implementation of faith. Without action, faith remains a mere concept, akin to daydreaming. There are many who hold beliefs but fail to act on them, resulting in unfulfilled potential and unrealized dreams. Applied faith, however, is an active, dynamic force. It's about taking concrete steps towards your goals, driven by your belief in their eventual realization.

In essence, the additional principles equip you with the

practical tools and mindset needed to transform your purpose, network, and faith into tangible results. They ensure that your journey is well-rounded and resilient, capable of withstanding and overcoming the inevitable challenges along the way. This comprehensive approach is what ultimately leads to sustained success and fulfillment.

FAITH AND THE FIRST THREE PRINCIPLES OF SUCCESS

1. **Definiteness of Purpose.** Definiteness of purpose is the cornerstone of all achievement. It is the clear and specific vision of what you intend to accomplish. This principle is supported by relentless personal initiative and action. Action, action, action—the more action, the better. It means continual and consistent effort, not just from you, but also from those who collaborate with you or your mastermind allies. When your purpose is definite, it becomes a guiding star, aligning your actions and the efforts of your team towards a common goal. This alignment amplifies the impact of each action, propelling you closer to success with every step you take.

2. **Positive Mental Attitude.** A positive mental attitude is indispensable. It is the foundation upon which faith is built. A positive mind, free from negatives such as fear, envy, hatred, jealousy, and greed, is crucial. Your mental attitude determines the effectiveness of your faith. This is a fact. The state of mind you are in when you pray or set your intentions will significantly influence the outcome. There is no ambiguity about it. You can test this principle for yourself and discover its validity. Reflect on your experiences—have you ever sent out prayers or intentions that resulted only in

disappointment or negative outcomes? This likely happened because you lacked absolute faith in your success. Unless you possess unwavering belief that you will achieve what you are aiming for, and can vividly see it in your possession before you even start asking for it, the impact of your prayer or intention is likely to be negative. Faith is an active force, and it requires a positive mental attitude to thrive.

3. **Mastermind Alliance.** A mastermind alliance is a critical principle. It involves bringing together one or more individuals who exude courage based on faith and who are mentally and spiritually aligned with your purpose. This alliance forms a collective mind, combining the knowledge, skills, and resources of each member to achieve a shared objective. The power of a mastermind group lies in its ability to multiply the potential of each individual. When people who share a common goal and a positive mental attitude come together, their combined efforts produce extraordinary results. This synergy is the essence of a mastermind alliance, and it plays a pivotal role in turning your definiteness of purpose into reality.

Faith is the thread that weaves these principles together. It is the mainspring of the soul, the driving force that translates your desires, plans, and purposes into tangible outcomes. Faith is not just a passive belief; it is an active, dynamic force that propels you into action. Without faith, your efforts may lack the conviction and persistence needed to achieve your goals. Applied faith is what turns your dreams into reality. It is the catalyst that transforms a definite purpose, a positive mental attitude, and a mastermind alliance into real-world success.

In essence, the first three principles of success—Definiteness of Purpose, Positive Mental Attitude, and Mastermind Alliance—

are fundamentally interconnected through the power of faith. These principles provide a solid foundation for achieving any goal, but they must be supported by additional principles to ensure comprehensive and sustained success. The other fourteen principles act as the necessary ingredients that complete the recipe for success, just as in baking a cake, where every ingredient plays a vital role. Together, these seventeen principles create a robust framework that guides you on your journey to success, ensuring that your efforts are well-rounded, resilient, and ultimately fruitful.

ELEMENTS OF APPLIED FAITH

Every Adversity Carries with It the Seed of an Equivalent Benefit

One of the core tenets of applied faith is the understanding that every adversity, every setback, carries within it the seed of an equivalent benefit. This principle is fundamental because it shifts the perspective on challenges and defeats. Temporary defeat is not failure until it is accepted as such. The majority of people falter in their application of faith when they encounter defeat and perceive it as insurmountable. Instead of seeking the hidden opportunity or lesson within the setback, they succumb to feelings of moodiness, brooding, and discouragement, ultimately fostering an inferiority complex.

However, this defeatist mindset can be transformed. When faced with adversity, the key is to immediately begin searching for the seed of an equivalent benefit. This proactive approach can reverse the negative spiral and turn defeat into a temporary setback, merely a point from which to launch another effort. My assertion that every adversity carries with it the seed of an equivalent benefit, and that every defeat and every failure contains such a seed, would hold little meaning without practical application and numerous illustrative examples.

If you reflect on enough examples from your own experiences, you will find that this principle consistently holds true. Consider times in your life when an apparent failure led to an unexpected opportunity or lesson that ultimately benefited you. By examining adversities closely, you can see the patterns and affirm this principle in action. This perspective encourages resilience and fosters a mindset that views challenges not as dead-ends but as stepping stones to greater achievements.

For instance, think back to a moment when you faced a significant setback in your career or personal life. Initially, it may have seemed like a complete failure, a moment of despair. But with time, perhaps you realized that this setback taught you a valuable lesson, introduced you to new opportunities, or redirected your path in a more favorable direction. These experiences illustrate that within each adversity lies the potential for growth and benefit. By embracing this principle, you cultivate the strength to see beyond immediate disappointments and to recognize the latent potential within each challenge. This mindset not only empowers you to persevere but also enhances your ability to innovate and adapt. Thus, the seed of an equivalent benefit becomes a powerful tool in your journey of applied faith, transforming setbacks into catalysts for progress.

Do you realize that your adversities are often your greatest blessings? For example, the greatest blessing that ever came into my life was, paradoxically, the loss of my mother. Typically, the greatest catastrophe that could befall a child is losing their mother at the tender age of nine.

Why do I say this was the greatest blessing? It's because her loss brought a new mother into my life, one who profoundly influenced everything I have achieved and everything I shall achieve. Without her guidance and influence, I might still be entangled in the destructive lifestyle that characterized my relatives—fighting rattlesnakes, drinking mountain liquor, and engaging in feuds. My relatives continue to live that way, so there is little reason to believe I would have escaped that fate without her intervention. I have faced many other adversities, and without these twenty major challenges, I would never have developed the depth of understanding required to appreciate the philosophy that every adversity contains the seed of an equivalent benefit.

Consider another profound adversity: being informed that my son was born without any signs of ears and was expected to be deaf and mute for his entire life. Can you imagine anything more devastating? Yet, I am forever thankful because my connection with Infinite Intelligence provided my son with a partial hearing system, granting him 65 percent of his normal hearing, and eventually, with modern hearing aids, 100 percent. He learned to live a normal life, and this experience provided me with the most powerful demonstration of faith's power I have ever encountered. I couldn't have understood this principle secondhand; I had to experience it firsthand.

I never accepted my son's affliction, not even before I saw him, and certainly not after. While his relatives accepted it and wanted to place him in a school for the underprivileged where he would learn sign language and lip reading, I refused to let him even know such things existed. When he was old enough for school, I fought the authorities every year to prevent him from being sent to a school for underprivileged children. I didn't want him exposed to others' afflictions. Instead, I taught him from the beginning that his lack of ears was a great blessing, and he believed it.

This belief led others to show him compassion and do things for him they wouldn't have done otherwise. For example, he got a job as a salesman for the Saturday Evening Post and became the top salesman in the United States. Often, he would go out with five dollars' worth of merchandise and come back with ten dollars in cash. People would see him and think, 'That poor little fellow with no ears is out selling papers. His parents must be poor.' They'd give him a dollar bill and refuse change, saying, 'Oh, sonny, you just keep that.' Consequently, he frequently earned a dollar per paper, far more than usual.

Today, my son lives a perfectly normal life, entirely unconcerned with any affliction because he was taught that any adversity can be transmuted into a benefit. This profound lesson underscores the incredible power of faith and positive perception. By reframing challenges and adversities as opportunities for growth and blessings in disguise, we can transform our lives and those of others. The ability to see the seed of benefit in every adversity is not just a philosophical stance but a practical approach to overcoming life's inevitable hurdles.

Applied Faith Requires the Habit of Affirming One's Definite Major Purpose in the Form of a Prayer at Least Once Daily.

Applied faith is an active, deliberate practice. One of its essential components is the daily affirmation of your definite major purpose, ideally framed as a prayer or positive declaration. This practice is crucial because the subconscious mind operates on the information it receives, whether it is truth or falsehood, positive or negative. The subconscious mind does not discriminate between a lie and the truth, nor does it differentiate between a penny and a million dollars. It simply absorbs and acts upon the dominant thoughts that you impress upon it.

Consider this: if you constantly feed your subconscious mind thoughts of poverty, ill health, and failure, it will respond accordingly. Your life will reflect these negative inputs, regardless of any faith you may try to muster later on. The subconscious mind responds to the mental attitude you maintain throughout the day, so it's imperative to continually affirm your goals and desires.

Affirming your definite major purpose is about more than just casual repetition. It's about engaging with your goals deeply and consistently until your subconscious mind is fully educated to automatically attract the resources, opportunities, and circumstances that align with your aims. By repeatedly affirming what you intend to achieve, you imprint these desires onto your subconscious, turning them into a powerful magnet that draws the necessary elements into your life.

Imagine your mind as an electrode magnet. When you charge it with a vivid and clear picture of what you want to achieve, it starts to attract everything related to that goal from the highways and byways of life. This magnetic effect is the result of the law of attraction, where like attracts like. Your focused, repeated affirmations create a mental state that magnetizes and pulls in people, opportunities, and resources that align with your objectives.

For instance, if your definite major purpose is to become a successful entrepreneur, you would affirm this goal daily with specific, positive statements such as, 'I am a successful entrepreneur. I attract profitable opportunities and create value in the marketplace.' Over time, these affirmations seep into your subconscious, influencing your thoughts, actions, and even your external circumstances. Moreover, this daily practice of affirmation builds resilience and fortifies your faith. It acts as a shield against negative influences and helps maintain a positive mental attitude, which is crucial for navigating life's challenges. When setbacks occur, your ingrained affirmations help you to see them not as failures, but as temporary obstacles that can be overcome.

In practical terms, start by dedicating a quiet moment each day to focus on your affirmations. Close your eyes, take a few deep breaths, and visualize your goals as if they are already accomplished. Speak your affirmations with conviction and emotion, as if you truly believe in their eventual manifestation. This daily ritual reinforces your commitment to your goals and solidifies your faith in their attainment.

Over time, you will notice a shift in your mindset and circumstances. The consistent practice of affirming your definite major purpose transforms your subconscious into a powerful ally, working tirelessly behind the scenes to align your reality with your aspirations. This is the essence of applied faith—harnessing the power of your mind to create the life you desire through deliberate, focused, and persistent affirmation.

Recognition of the Existence of an Infinite Intelligence

A crucial element of applied faith is the recognition of an Infinite Intelligence that orchestrates the vast and intricate order of the entire universe. This concept is foundational, as it affirms that you are a minute expression of this boundless intelligence. As such, your mind has no inherent limitations except those that you accept or establish within yourself. Let me emphasize this point: your mind has no limitations whatsoever, except those you allow to be imposed or that you deliberately set up.

This is a profound statement, but the accomplishments of individuals like Thomas Edison, Henry Ford, Andrew Carnegie, and even Napoleon Hill illustrate that the only limits are those we accept. These luminaries achieved extraordinary feats not because they were inherently more brilliant or intelligent than the average person, but because they believed in their capacity to achieve and never wavered in their belief.

Consider my own journey. If I had ever doubted for even a second my ability to achieve my goals—from the time I began working with Mr. Carnegie to the moment I presented this philosophy to the world—I would never have succeeded. How did I accomplish it? It wasn't due to exceptional brilliance or superior intelligence. I possess no more brilliance or intelligence than the average person. My success hinged on unwavering belief. The harder the challenges I faced, the stronger my belief in my ability to overcome them became. This steadfast belief, especially in the face of adversity, exemplifies applied faith.

Applied faith requires you to believe in yourself, particularly during testing times. When adversity strikes or people oppose you, it is crucial to side with yourself and maintain your faith. Do not succumb to self-doubt. This internal solidarity and unwavering belief in your potential are the essence of applied faith. You must embrace this attitude fully.

Testing times are an inevitable part of life. No one attains a high position or success without facing trials and tests. You are not allowed to climb to the top without proving your worth at lower levels first. This gradual progression ensures that you earn your position through perseverance and resilience. Observing this natural order, it becomes evident that the Creator, or Infinite Intelligence, subjects everyone to tests to validate their readiness for higher stages in life. Although we may not fully comprehend the Creator's methods, we can see a clear pattern: severe testing is a prerequisite for attaining and maintaining elevated positions in life.

These tests are not arbitrary; they are essential for growth and development. Each challenge and setback serves as an opportunity to strengthen your character and resolve. By overcoming these obstacles, you demonstrate your capability and readiness for greater responsibilities and achievements. This process ensures that only those who are truly prepared and deserving rise to the top.

In conclusion, recognizing the existence of an Infinite Intelligence and understanding your connection to it is vital for applied faith. This recognition empowers you to break free from self-imposed limitations and believe in your boundless potential. By maintaining unwavering belief in yourself, especially during testing times, you harness the power of applied faith to achieve your goals and fulfill your purpose. Embrace this principle, and you will find that no obstacle is insurmountable and no dream unattainable.

One of the most striking findings from my research is that individuals who achieve great things in various fields, throughout history, have done so in direct proportion to the amount of defeat and opposition they faced. This remarkable correlation suggests that greatness is intrinsically linked to the struggles and adversities one overcomes. It's no coincidence that every one of these extraordinary individuals became great precisely because they were once small, faced significant opposition, and had to struggle mightily to achieve their goals.

In my own experience, I have often shared the story of my early struggles and numerous defeats. Although my business manager advised against it, believing it might not be wise to reveal such vulnerabilities, I firmly believe it is beneficial. By sharing my hardships and the resilience required to keep moving forward, I aim to inspire others. If you understand the magnitude of the challenges I faced and see how I managed to rise above them and live to deliver this philosophy, you might say, 'If

Hill can do it, I can do it too.' This is the primary reason I speak about my defeats—so that others can draw strength and motivation from my experiences.

When discussing the concept of a higher power or guiding force, it doesn't matter which term you use—God, Jehovah, Buddha, or Muhammad. We are all referring to one fundamental cause, the singular source responsible for the universe, for you, for me, and for everything that exists. There cannot be two first causes; there is only one. I choose to call it Infinite Intelligence, a term that is neutral and inclusive, appealing to students of all faiths and religions around the world.

Believing in this Infinite Intelligence is crucial, but belief alone is not enough. You must be able to prove to yourself and provide concrete evidence that this first cause exists and that you can draw upon its power. Without this deep-seated conviction and tangible proof, you won't be able to make full use of a definite plan for your life.

To illustrate, think about how Edison, Ford, Carnegie, and other great achievers spoke of their belief in a higher power that guided their actions and decisions. This belief wasn't abstract or superficial; it was a profound certainty that fueled their perseverance and innovation. They didn't just hope for success—they believed with unwavering conviction that they were part of a grand design and could tap into this Infinite Intelligence to overcome any obstacle.

In practical terms, this means developing a habit of daily affirmations and visualizations that reinforce your connection to this Infinite Intelligence. Write down your goals, visualize your success, and affirm your belief in the support and guidance of this higher power. This practice strengthens your faith and aligns your subconscious mind with your conscious desires, creating a powerful synergy that propels you toward your goals.

Moreover, recognizing the role of Infinite Intelligence in your life encourages humility and gratitude. It reminds you that you are part of a larger, interconnected universe, and that your achievements are not solely the result of your efforts but also the manifestation of a greater plan. This perspective fosters resilience, as you understand that setbacks and failures are not the end but part of the journey toward greater accomplishments.

The recognition of an Infinite Intelligence and the belief in your ability to draw upon this source is fundamental to achieving greatness. By embracing this belief, proving it to yourself, and incorporating it into your daily practices, you align yourself with the natural order of the universe. This alignment empowers you to overcome adversity, persist through challenges, and ultimately realize your definite major purpose. Through this process, you become a living testament to the power of applied faith, demonstrating that no obstacle is insurmountable and no goal is unattainable when you believe in the limitless potential within and around you.

One of my students once asked me about my concept of Infinite Intelligence and whether it was synonymous with God. I responded affirmatively, saying, 'Yes, I do mean the same thing.' The student then inquired, 'Can you prove the existence of your concept of God?' My answer was rooted in the observable universe: 'Everything in the universe serves as the finest evidence of Its existence, particularly because of the orderliness found throughout the cosmos.'

Indeed, the universe's remarkable orderliness stands as a testament to a first cause, an Infinite Intelligence. From the smallest particles, like electrons and protons, to the grandest celestial bodies floating through space, everything operates in perfect harmony. There is no chaos, no planets colliding randomly. The precision with which the universe functions—from the atomic level to the cosmic scale—provides compelling evidence of a guiding intelligence. In fact, there is more evidence supporting the existence of a first cause than nearly anything else we can observe.

However, if you choose not to believe in this, if you do not accept it, see it, feel it, and know it, then you miss out on recognizing that you are a minute part of that Infinite Intelligence. This intelligence is expressed through your brain, and acknowledging this fact is crucial. It leads to the profound understanding that your only limitations are those you impose on yourself, or those you allow others or circumstances to impose upon you.

Taking a careful inventory of your past defeats and the adversities they brought reveals a powerful truth: all such experiences carry the seed of an equivalent benefit. Each setback and challenge is not merely an obstacle but a potential source of growth and learning. This concept aligns with the idea of Infinite Intelligence, suggesting that every difficulty we face has a purpose and can lead to positive outcomes if we approach it with the right mindset. For example, consider the rigorous trials faced by great inventors and leaders throughout history. Thomas Edison, who faced countless failures before perfecting the electric light bulb, famously viewed each failure as a step closer to success. His persistence and belief in a higher order guiding his work exemplify how recognizing and tapping into Infinite Intelligence can lead to remarkable achievements. Similarly, Henry Ford faced numerous setbacks before revolutionizing the automobile industry. His unwavering belief in his vision, despite initial failures, demonstrates the power of applied faith and the recognition of an organizing intelligence that helps transform adversity into triumph.

In your own life, embracing this concept means consistently affirming your goals and maintaining a positive mental attitude. It involves daily practices that reinforce your connection to Infinite Intelligence, such as visualization, prayer, or meditation. By doing so, you align your subconscious mind with your conscious desires, creating a powerful force that attracts the resources and opportunities needed to achieve your goals. This perspective fosters resilience and perseverance. When faced with adversity, instead of succumbing to defeat, you look for the seed of benefit hidden within the challenge. This shift in mindset transforms setbacks into valuable learning experiences and stepping stones toward your ultimate success.

In conclusion, the recognition of Infinite Intelligence as synonymous with God, and the understanding of your integral part in this grand design, empowers you to transcend self-imposed limitations. By accepting that everything in the universe, including your own mind, operates under this intelligent order, you harness the power to turn every defeat into a benefit. This approach not only leads to personal growth and achievement but also aligns you with the natural harmony of the universe, enabling you to fulfill your highest potential.

PART III

People Skills for Stellar Success

7

Plotting Your Course to Greatness

The mind of man would indeed surpass all other Miracles of Life if ranked by importance, because it is the instrument through which man connects himself to all things and circumstances that influence his life. Without a doubt, the human mind is the most mysterious and awe-inspiring product of nature, yet it remains the least understood and most frequently misused of man's profound gifts from the Creator.

The mind serves as the citadel of the soul, where the link between man's conscious thought and Infinite Intelligence resides. It acts as the switchboard, allowing man to tune in and directly communicate with the vast universal reservoir of Infinite Intelligence, seeking answers to his problems and the fulfillment of his dreams and aspirations.

Most significantly, the mind is the sole entity over which the Creator has given man complete control—a prerogative not even the Creator has revoked or altered, suggesting the mind was intended exclusively for man's use. It stands as the most crucial of all gifts from the Creator, empowering man to shape much of his earthly destiny.

Successes and failures in life stem directly from how man uses—or neglects to use—his mind. The mind's functions can be categorized into nine departments, akin to a well-organized business. Some operate automatically, independent of individual direction, while others remain under constant individual control.

Here's a breakdown of the mind's departments:

(a) The Faculty of Will: Will acts as the overseer of all other departments of the mind. It is where the individual exercises the Great Prerogative of exclusive control over his thoughts. It executes the individual's commands, regardless of their nature or consequences. Its strength correlates directly with its use; an idle Will, like an idle arm, grows weak and ineffective.

(b) The Faculty of Reason: Reason serves as the judge within the mind. When allowed, it evaluates all ideas, goals, desires, and circumstances presented to it. However, its decisions can be overridden by the Will or influenced by emotions if the Will does not assert itself. One common pitfall in thinking is letting emotions override the Will, which can lead to tragic outcomes, as emotions do not align with logic or reason.

(c) The Faculty of Emotions: Emotions often initiate much of the mind's activity. People frequently make decisions based on their feelings without the oversight of Reason and Will. Such decisions tend to be more unsound than sound. Love, in particular, a powerful emotion, can lead to significant consequences when not tempered by Reason and Will.

Accurate thinkers, who utilize all departments of their mind, refrain from allowing Love to dictate actions until reviewed by Reason and Will. They subject their deepest desires and plans to Reason and Will to ensure enthusiasm does not outweigh wisdom.

(d) The Faculty of Imagination: Imagination serves as the architect of man's destiny, allowing him to shape and reshape his life as desired. It empowers man to explore limitless possibilities and innovate new ideas and concepts. However, uncontrolled imagination can wreak havoc, especially when combined with unchecked emotions like love. Imagination can lead to hypochondria or even cure it, illustrating its profound influence over the physical body. Its potential is vast yet requires constant supervision by Reason and Will.

(e) The Faculty of Conscience: Conscience provides moral guidance, evaluating whether one's aims and purposes align with natural moral laws. When heeded, it grants the faith needed to achieve one's goals.

(f) The Five Physical Senses: Sight, sound, taste, smell, and touch are the mind's means of interfacing with the external world and acquiring information. However, their reliability fluctuates, necessitating oversight by Reason and Will to avoid decisions influenced by fear or anger.

(g) The Faculty of Memory: Memory serves as the brain's filing cabinet, storing all thoughts, experiences, and sensations received through the senses. Its reliability varies and requires discipline and supervision by Will and Reason to function effectively.

(h) The Sixth Sense: This serves as the mind's broadcasting and receiving station, enabling communication through thought vibrations, including telepathy. It connects individuals with unseen guides and higher planes of intelligence beyond Earth.

(i) The Subconscious Section of the Mind: This serves as the switchboard connecting the conscious mind with Infinite Intelligence. It acts upon ideas and plans sent to it, regardless of their nature, responding more effectively to highly emotionalized inputs. It requires overcoming barriers set by the conscious mind to operate optimally.

This overview of the mind's departments offers a high-level view of its operation, emphasizing that all thoughts, positive or negative, manifest physically. They inspire ideas and plans that align with desired ends through natural and logical means, shaping one's reality.

While 'thoughts are things' remains debatable, it is clear that thoughts create things, reflecting their nature. Many believe every released thought initiates a vibration that returns to its originator. Man, as a physical manifestation, mirrors thoughts put into motion by Infinite Intelligence, with human thought energy being a projection of the universal source through the brain's apparatus.

THE SUBCONSCIOUS MIND WILL NOT ACT UPON ANY IDEA, PLAN, OR PURPOSE WHICH IS NOT CLEARLY EXPRESSED TO IT.

Therefore, clarity and precision in communicating with the Subconscious mind are paramount for achieving desired outcomes. It acts as a bridge between the conscious mind and Infinite Intelligence, manifesting ideas and intentions into reality when properly directed and managed.

Each aspect of the mind—Will, Reason, Emotions, Imagination, Conscience, Senses, Memory, Sixth Sense, and Subconscious—plays a crucial role in the holistic functioning of human consciousness. Together, they form a complex yet interconnected system that governs thought, perception, decision-making, and ultimately, the course of one's life.

Understanding and mastering these faculties is not merely a theoretical exercise but a practical necessity for anyone seeking to optimize their mental potential and achieve personal and spiritual growth. It requires discipline, self-awareness, and a commitment to harnessing the power of the mind in alignment with higher principles and values.

In conclusion, the mind stands as humanity's greatest asset and responsibility—a tool with the power to shape individual destinies and contribute to the greater tapestry of universal consciousness. How we choose to use this gift, entrusted to us by the Creator, defines not only our personal success and fulfillment but also our collective journey toward understanding and realizing our true potential.

The exploration of the mind's capabilities continues to be a journey of discovery and enlightenment, offering infinite possibilities for those willing to delve deeper into its mysteries and unleash its boundless potential for creativity, innovation, and profound transformation in both personal and collective realms.

In essence, the mind's depth and complexity invite continual exploration and understanding, encouraging individuals to cultivate a harmonious relationship with its faculties. By nurturing and refining these faculties—Will, Reason, Emotions, Imagination, Conscience, Senses, Memory, Sixth Sense, and Subconscious—we expand our capacity to shape our realities consciously and participate meaningfully in the unfolding story of human existence.

8

Dancing in the Rain

'You are a mind with a body!'
Because you are a mind, you possess mystical powers—both those recognized and those yet to be discovered. Dare to explore the powers of your mind! Why explore them?

When you uncover the truths that await you, they can bring you: (1) physical, mental, and moral health, happiness, and wealth; (2) success in your chosen field of endeavor; and even (3) a means to harness, utilize, control, or harmonize with powers, whether known or unknown.

And dare to investigate all non-physical forces lying beyond the realm of known physical processes—forces that you can wield once you learn how to apply them. And this will not prove too difficult for you—no more challenging than switching on a television set for the first time.

Just as a young child can tune into their favorite television program without understanding the workings of the broadcasting station or their receiver, so too can you. What matters is knowing how to turn the right knob or press the right button.

In this chapter, you'll discover how to manipulate the

intricate mechanisms of the most powerful electrical device ever conceived. Though this remarkable machine is the sublime creation of Divine Power, it belongs to you. How is it crafted? Well, it consists of over 80 trillion electrical cells among other components, each functioning as its own electrical mechanism.

One particular marvel weighs a mere fifty ounces yet comprises over 10 billion cells that generate, receive, record, and transmit energy.

What is this incredible machine that you possess? It's your body. Even if you lose an arm, an eye, or other parts, you remain fundamentally yourself.

And the astonishing marvel? Your brain and nervous system—the mechanism that controls your body and facilitates your mind's activities.

Speaking of your mind: it, too, has components—the conscious and the subconscious—working in sync. While scientists have made significant strides in understanding the conscious mind, it's been less than a century since we began exploring the vast, mysterious realm of the subconscious. Primitive humans have long utilized the mystical powers of the subconscious, a practice that continues today among groups like the Aborigines of Australia and other indigenous peoples.

LET'S START EXPLORING NOW!

At the tender age of 19, Bill ventured into his first business—hides and skins—but met with failure. Undeterred, at 21, he ran for Federal Congress, only to face disappointment once more. Instead of crushing him, these setbacks ignited a fire within Bill, sparking what he termed 'inspirational dissatisfaction.'

Driven by a quest for success, Bill delved into the study of principles that govern wealth. His search led him to the shelves of inspirational books in the library, where the title *Think and Grow Rich* caught his eye. Borrowing the book, he immersed himself in its teachings, reading it repeatedly. Yet, despite multiple readings, the practical application of the principles eluded him.

It was during his fourth reading, strolling down a Sydney business street, that inspiration struck. Standing before a meat market window, Bill had a sudden epiphany. He recalled: 'That's it! I've got it!' His outburst startled a passing lady, but he rushed home with newfound clarity.

Reflecting on Chapter Four of *Think and Grow Rich*, titled 'Autosuggestion: The Medium for Influencing the Subconscious Mind,' Bill remembered his father's readings from Emile Coué's 'Self-Mastery Through Conscious Autosuggestion' during his childhood. He realized the potential of autosuggestion not just for health but also for acquiring wealth—a revelation that felt entirely new.

Bill enthusiastically recounted the principles as if reciting them from memory, affirming his belief in the power of autosuggestion to manifest riches and any other desired outcome.

'You know, conscious autosuggestion is the mechanism through which an individual can deliberately nourish his subconscious mind with thoughts of a creative nature, or, by neglect, allow thoughts of a destructive nature to take root in the fertile soil of his mind.

When you read aloud twice daily the written statement of your desire for money with emotion and focused attention, and you vividly imagine yourself already in possession of that money, you effectively communicate your desire directly to your subconscious mind. Through consistently repeating this process, you establish thought patterns that support your efforts to transform desire into tangible wealth.

Let me emphasize again: It is crucial that when you read aloud your statement of desire to cultivate a money-consciousness, you do so with passion and intense feeling.

Your ability to harness the principles of autosuggestion hinges largely on your ability to concentrate on a specific desire until it becomes a burning obsession.

When I rushed home, breathless from running, I immediately sat down at the dining table and wrote: "My definite major aim is to be a millionaire by 1960." Looking directly at Napoleon Hill, he continued, "As you advised, one should specify the exact amount of money desired and set a deadline. I followed your guidance."'

The man we spoke with was no longer the young Bill McCall who faced setbacks at 19. He had become the Honorable William V. McCall, the youngest person ever elected to the Australian Parliament. He served as chairman of the board of directors of a Coca-Cola subsidiary in Sydney and directed 22 family-owned corporations. Regarding wealth—he achieved millionaire status, surpassing the men whose stories inspired him to explore the power of his subconscious mind through self-suggestion. (Interestingly, he reached millionaire status four years ahead of his scheduled target!)

'Day by day, in every way, I am getting better and better!' Note how we use 'self-suggestion' as synonymous with 'conscious autosuggestion,' as used by Emile Coué.

McCall recalled that in his youth, his father had benefited greatly from a discovery found in a book of his time—a discovery that any man, woman, or child can effectively employ when they discover it for themselves. Like Bill McCall and his father, you too can harness the power of conscious autosuggestion.

CONSCIOUS SUGGESTION

Emile Coué uncovered conscious autosuggestion through his exploration of his own mind and the minds of others. Before his breakthrough, he utilized hypnosis to treat his patients' physical ailments. However, once he made his pivotal discovery, rooted in a simple natural law, he abandoned hypnosis altogether.

How did he identify and grasp this natural law?

Emile Coué's breakthrough came when he found answers to several questions he posed to himself:

Question 1: Is it the doctor's suggestion or the patient's suggestion that brings about healing?

Answer: Coué definitively proved that it is the patient's own mind, whether subconsciously or consciously, that generates the suggestion to which their mind and body respond. Without either unconscious autosuggestion or conscious autosuggestion, external suggestions are ineffective.

Question 2: If the doctor's suggestion triggers the patient's internal suggestion, why can't the patient use positive, health-promoting suggestions on themselves? And why can't they refrain from harmful, negative suggestions?

The answer to his second question became clear: Anyone, even a child, can be taught to cultivate a positive mental attitude. The method involves repeating positive affirmations such as: 'Day by day, in every way, through the grace of God, I am getting better and better.'

When death's door is on the verge of opening, stark realities emerge. Annually, more than 450,000 children are born out of wedlock in the United States, while over one and a half million teenagers find themselves incarcerated for crimes like car theft. These personal tragedies could often be prevented if (a) parents learned the art of effective suggestion, and (b) their sons and daughters were taught to harness the power of spiritual self-suggestion. Through proper guidance in suggestion, these young individuals could be inspired to cultivate unwavering moral principles through their own conscious autosuggestion. They would also be equipped to intelligently counter or deflect negative influences from their peers.

Certainly, throughout life, every person responds more frequently to unconscious autosuggestion than to conscious autosuggestion. In such instances, responses are driven by habit and the subconscious's inner promptings. When an individual with a Positive Mental Attitude (PMA) faces a significant personal crisis, self-motivators from the subconscious mind often emerge to aid them. This phenomenon is particularly pronounced in emergencies—such as when Ralph Weppner, a student in our PMA Science of Success course from Toowoomba, Queensland, Australia, found himself in dire circumstances.

It was 1:30 in the morning in a small hospital room where two nursing sisters maintained a watchful presence beside Ralph's bed. The previous afternoon at 4:30, an urgent call had summoned his family to the hospital. Upon arrival, they found Ralph in a coma following a severe heart attack. Now, they stood in the corridor, each engaged in their own mix of worry and prayer.

In the dimly lit bedroom, two nursing sisters worked anxiously, each monitoring one of Ralph's wrists, attempting to detect any pulse. Ralph had remained in a coma for a full six-hour period, and after the doctor had exhausted all possible efforts and left the room to attend to another critical patient elsewhere in the hospital, the atmosphere was tense.

Unable to move, speak, or feel anything, Ralph was nonetheless conscious and could hear the voices of the sisters clearly. He listened as one of them exclaimed with concern, 'He's not breathing! Can you detect a pulse?' The reply came back, 'No.'

Repeatedly, he heard the same question and response: 'Can you detect a pulse now?' 'No.'

Internally composed and somewhat amused by the sisters' reactions, Ralph thought to himself, 'I'm perfectly fine. I'm not going to die. But how can I communicate this to them?'

Recalling a self-motivational technique he had learned, he affirmed to himself, 'You can do it if you believe you can!'

Struggling against his physical limitations, Ralph attempted to open his eyes, but his efforts seemed futile as his eyelids refused to obey his command. He tried to move his limbs and head, yet he felt no response whatsoever. Despite the lack of sensation, he persisted in trying to open his eyes until he finally heard a glimmer of hope in the sisters' voices: 'I saw one eyelid flicker—he's still there.'

Reflecting on the experience, Ralph later recounted, 'I felt no fear and found the situation somewhat amusing. Periodically, one sister would call out to me, 'Are you there, Mr. Weppner? Are you there?' Each time, I attempted to respond by moving my eyelid, signaling to them that I was alright—I was still present.'

This continued for a significant period until Ralph, through relentless effort, finally managed to open one eye, and then both. At that moment, his doctor returned, demonstrating remarkable skill and persistence along with the nurses, who successfully revived him.

The autosuggestion Ralph had memorized from the PMA Science of Success course—'You can do it if you believe you can'—played a pivotal role in his miraculous recovery from death's door.

THE HIDDEN FORCES

The books we read and the thoughts we entertain exert a profound influence on our subconscious minds. Yet, there exist unseen forces that also wield significant power, operating below the threshold of consciousness.

These unseen forces may originate from known physical causes or from sources that remain mysterious. To illustrate this, consider a well-documented example that gained widespread attention following Vance Packard's book *Hidden Persuaders*. This story was initially reported in American newspapers and later featured in magazines, detailing an experiment in a New Jersey movie theater involving subliminal advertising.

Over a six-week period, more than forty thousand moviegoers unwittingly became participants in an experiment where advertising messages were flashed on the screen at speeds too fast for conscious awareness. These messages promoted products available in the theater lobby. At the conclusion of the experiment, the results were astonishing: sales of one product surged by more than 50%, while another product saw an increase of nearly 20%.

The inventor of the process explained that despite the invisibility of the messages, they still had a profound impact on many in the audience due to the subconscious mind's ability to absorb fleeting impressions that escape conscious registration.

When this story surfaced in the media, the public reacted with horror at the attempt to influence their thinking patterns, purchasing decisions, and thought processes through subliminal suggestion. There was widespread fear of subtle forms of brainwashing. However, it's noteworthy that the principles of Positive Mental Attitude (PMA) offer an alternative perspective. Subliminal suggestion can be harnessed for positive purposes as well. Just as power can be used for both good and evil depending on its direction, so too can subconscious influences be employed for constructive ends.

Now that the experiment has demonstrated its potential impact, one can easily envision the beneficial effects if the following self-motivators were flashed on a movie screen:

- God is always a good God!
- Day by day, in every way, through the grace of God, you are getting better and better!
- Have the courage to face the truth!
- What the mind of man can conceive and believe, the mind of man can achieve with PMA!
- Every adversity has the seed of an equivalent or greater benefit for those who have a positive mental attitude!
- You can do it if you believe you can!

The PMA approach mentioned would indeed be effective if the audience's consent was obtained beforehand.

Another example of a known physical force affecting the subconscious mind can be seen in the impact of radar on navigators. The sinking incidents involving the SS Andrea Doria and SS Valchem raise questions about radar's role. The collision between the Andrea Doria and the Stockholm, and the Santa Rosa with the Valchem, resulted in fatalities despite radar detection. Radar waves potentially played a significant role, though investigations into the true causes of these collisions have not yielded definitive answers.

Sidney A. Schneider, from Skokie, Illinois, developed a keen interest in hypnotism as a teenager, inspired by his brother's success with it. Later in his career, as an expert hypnotist and electronics engineer, Schneider worked on radar systems during World War II, specifically with the I. F. F. (Information, Friend or Foe) system. He observed that radar operators sometimes entered trances without realizing it, which he attributed to the synchronization of radar waves with brain waves. Schneider's understanding of hypnosis and electronics led him to modify radar waves to prevent these trances from recurring among naval personnel.

BRAIN WAVE SYNCHRONIZER

What is the Brain Wave Synchronizer? It is an electronic instrument designed to induce various levels of hypnosis through subliminal and photic (light) stimulation of brain waves. The device can operate independently or in conjunction with a therapist's recorded verbal suggestions. No physical connections or attachments are required on the patient. Effective results can be achieved at distances where the machine's light is visible. The apparatus induces hypnotic states from light to deep levels in over 90 percent of subjects within an average of three minutes.

In an experimental setting with the Brain Wave Synchronizer, participants were unaware of the machine's capabilities or that they were part of an experiment. Nevertheless, 30 percent of them experienced varying degrees of hypnosis, ranging from light to deep states.

'Why and how does the Brain Wave Synchronizer function?' we inquired. 'It operates akin to a television transmitter,' explained Schneider. 'The human brain emits electric pulses (waves) across different frequency ranges. This understanding has been applied in medical practice since 1929 with the development of the electroencephalograph, commonly known as the EEG machine, used to record brain waves.'

'My machine functions much like a television system,' Schneider elaborated. 'The reason the picture on your television set remains steady is due to the pulses generated within the set synchronizing with those from the transmitting station. The receiver operates at a rate dictated by the transmitter, ensuring a stable picture.

'Similarly, the Brain Wave Synchronizer generates synchronizing pulses. Through photic stimulation, these waves induce the brain's frequency to synchronize accordingly. This synchronization is pivotal for achieving hypnosis.

'Just as you compare your brain to a receiving set, think of the Brain Wave Synchronizer as a television transmitter.'

As you read further, you'll find that aside from likening your brain to a receiving set, you can also draw parallels to it being a television transmitter.

A little knowledge becomes a dangerous thing. Having explored some of the unseen forces from known physical causes, let's now delve deeper into the unknown: the fascinating realm of psychic phenomena, including:

1. **ESP (extrasensory perception)**: Awareness or response to external events not perceived through the senses. This includes:
    - **Telepathy**: Thought transference
    - **Clairvoyance**: Perception of objects not present to the senses
    - **Precognition**: Seeing into the future
    - **Postcognition**: Seeing into the past
2. **Psychokinesis**: The influence of the mind on an object.

Let's stay grounded in reality and approach the unknown with common sense! It's crucial to maintain logical thinking and avoid letting our minds gather cobwebs of uncertainty. Facts should guide us safely across the river of doubt. Therefore, it's wise to follow the guidance of experienced mentors who can lead us along secure paths. We'll introduce you to such a guide shortly. But first, let's reflect on the past.

Thomas J. Hudson's renowned book, *The Law of Psychic Phenomena*, published in 1893, became a bestseller. Even today, it continues to captivate readers, available in paperback through Kessinger Publishing in Whitefish, Montana. This book contained numerous gripping accounts of reported psychic experiences, stimulating the imaginations of tens of thousands. Some were prepared for this exploration; others were not.

Public interest in psychic phenomena surged thereafter, yet many individuals, lacking proper preparation, risked harm by delving into these powers without sufficient knowledge. A little understanding of psychic abilities can evoke awe and intense interest, sometimes leading to imprudent actions. It's understandable why many religious leaders, scientists, and those concerned with public welfare viewed the study of psychic phenomena with apprehension:

1. Imaginations could run wild, threatening mental stability.
2. Distinguishing fact from fiction became challenging.
3. Amateurs, vaudeville entertainers, and fraudulent individuals exploited hypnotism, mediums, and charlatans, misleading the public.
4. Fundamental religious principles could be distorted, leading to harmful paths.

Anything connected to psychic phenomena became stigmatized and taboo. Despite these risks and social stigmas, courageous and sensible individuals dared to seek the truth, guided by good judgment and integrity.

But it was left to the persistent efforts of Dr. Joseph Banks Rhine, formerly of Duke University, supported by his wife Dr. Louisa E. Rhine, to elevate the study of psychic phenomena to a position of respectability. Dr. Rhine's impeccable character and three decades of meticulously controlled laboratory experiments, governed by mathematical principles, were instrumental in this endeavor. His task was challenging because spontaneous psychic phenomena rarely manifest in laboratory settings. They typically occur unexpectedly, often during periods of intense emotional stress or heightened obsession, frequently coinciding with the death of a loved one.

Today, any writer delving into psychic phenomena seeks to bolster their credibility by referencing Dr. Rhine and Duke University. We are no different in this regard. We strongly recommend further exploration through Dr. Rhine's works, such as *The Reach of the Mind* and others authored or co-authored by him. Our advice: Let Dr. Joseph Banks Rhine be your guide.

How successful has Dr. Rhine been in breaking down skepticism and fostering belief in these extraordinary mental powers? A telling measure lies in the fact that pragmatic businessmen have been convinced and are conducting their own experiments. In an interview, Dr. Peter A. Castruccio, Director of the Westinghouse Astronautics Institute, affirmed that Westinghouse scientists are actively researching ways to utilize telepathy and clairvoyance for long-distance communication. Dr. Castruccio extensively consulted with Dr. Rhine before embarking on this ambitious project.

Will the pursuit of harnessing telepathy and clairvoyance for commercial viability prove successful? Consider this: Not long ago, concepts like converting matter into energy, atomic fission, artificial satellites, jet propulsion, and everyday technologies such as television were scoffed at as implausible.

Today, they are integral parts of our reality.

And what about the electronic computer, which was modeled after the human computer: the human brain and nervous system? Every one of these innovations was conceived, believed, and achieved by individuals with PMA! Machines capable of operating at the speed of light—186,300 miles per second! Machines that can perform 40,000 arithmetic operations per second and self-diagnose and correct errors! These machines became a reality because humans engineered them with electrical circuits that mimic the electrical activity found in the nervous system of your own body.

Our response remains: What the mind of man can conceive and believe, the mind of man can achieve with PMA!

Yet no machine or human invention can surpass the marvel of the incredible human computer you possess: your brain and nervous system, with their extraordinary electrical activity.

Man is not merely a body with a brain.

You are a mind with a body—a mind that possesses and is influenced by both known and unknown powers! A mind comprised of two parts: the conscious and the subconscious.

Here, we have emphasized the concept of the subconscious mind—its powers and the forces, known and unknown, that shape it. But what about the conscious mind? It is equally vital. You will delve into this further in the next chapter, aptly titled ... And Something More!

If your reaction to what you have read has sparked insight into how you can manipulate the right knob or push the right button to achieve your desires through the machine you own, then dare to explore the potentials of your mind. Let Pilot No. 4 guide you ... And Something More!

PART IV

Sustaining Lifelong Success

9

Crafting Bridges to Success

This lesson on initiative and leadership follows the lesson on self-confidence because no one can become an effective leader or take initiative in any significant undertaking without self-belief. Initiative and leadership are paired in this lesson because leadership is essential for achieving success, and initiative is the foundation upon which this vital quality of leadership is built. Initiative is as crucial to success as a hub is to a wagon wheel.

WHAT IS INITIATIVE?

It is that exceedingly rare quality that prompts—nay, impels—a person to do what ought to be done without being told. Elbert Hubbard eloquently addressed the subject of initiative, stating:

'The world bestows its big prizes, both in money and honors, for one thing, and that is Initiative. What is initiative? I'll tell you: It is doing the right thing without being told.

But next to doing the right thing without being told is to do it when you are told once. That is to say, "Carry the message to Garcia." Those who can carry a message get high honors, but their pay is not always in proportion.

Next, there are those who do the right thing when necessity kicks them from behind, and these get indifference instead of honors, and a pittance for pay. This kind spend most of their time polishing a bench with a hard luck story.

Then, still lower down in the scale than this, we have the fellow who will not do the right thing even when someone goes along to show him how and stays to see that he does it; he is always out of a job, and receives the contempt he deserves, unless he has a rich pa, in which case destiny patiently waits around the corner with a stuffed club.'

To which class do you belong?

Inasmuch as you will be expected to take inventory of yourself and determine which of the fifteen factors of this course you need most, after you have completed the sixteenth lesson, it may be well if you begin to get ready for this analysis by answering the question that Elbert Hubbard has asked: to which class do you belong?

One of the peculiarities of leadership is the fact that it is never found in those who have not acquired the habit of taking the initiative. Leadership is something that you must invite yourself into; it will never thrust itself upon you. If you carefully analyze all leaders whom you know, you will see that they not only exercised initiative, but they went about their work with a definite purpose in mind.

These facts are mentioned in this lesson for the reason that it will profit you to observe that successful people make use of all the factors covered by the sixteen lessons of the course; and, for the more important reason, that it will profit you to understand thoroughly the principle of organized effort which this Reading Course is intended to establish in your mind.

This seems an appropriate place to state that this course is not intended as a shortcut to success, nor is it intended as a mechanical formula that you may use in noteworthy achievement without effort on your part. The real value of the course lies in the use that you will make of it, and not in the course itself. The chief purpose of the course is to help you develop in yourself the fifteen qualities covered by the sixteen lessons of the course, and one of the most important of these qualities is Initiative, the subject of this lesson.

We will now proceed to apply the principle upon which this lesson is founded by describing, in detail, just how it served successfully to complete a business transaction that most people would call difficult.

In 1916, I needed $25,000 with which to create an educational institution, but I had neither this sum nor sufficient collateral with which to borrow it through the usual banking sources. Did I bemoan my fate or think of what I might accomplish if some rich relative or Good Samaritan would come to my rescue by loaning me the necessary capital?

I did nothing of the sort!

I did just what you will be advised, throughout this course, to do. First of all, I made the securing of this capital my definite chief aim. Second, I laid out a complete plan through which to transform this aim into reality. Backed by sufficient Self-confidence and spurred on by Initiative, I proceeded to put my plan into action. But, before the 'action' stage of the plan had been reached, more than six weeks of constant, persistent study and effort and thought were embodied in it. If a plan is to be sound, it must be built of carefully chosen material.

BECOMING AN INITIATOR

There are generally many plans through the operation of which a desired object may be achieved, and it often happens to be true that the obvious and usual methods employed are not the best. The usual method of procedure, in the case related, would have been that of borrowing from a bank. You can see that this method was impractical, in this case, for the reason that no collateral was available.

A great philosopher once said: 'Initiative is the pass-key that opens the door to opportunity.' I do not recall who this philosopher was, but I know that he was great because of the soundness of his statement.

We will now proceed to outline the exact procedure that you must follow if you are to become a person of initiative and leadership.

First: Master the Habit of Procrastination

You must master the habit of procrastination and eliminate it from your make-up. This habit of putting off until tomorrow that which you should have done last week, last year, or even decades ago is gnawing at the very vitals of your being. You can accomplish nothing until you throw it off. The method through which you eliminate procrastination is based upon a well-known and scientifically tested principle of psychology which has been referred to in the two preceding lessons of this course as auto-suggestion.

Copy the following formula and place it conspicuously in your room where you will see it as you retire at night and as you arise in the morning.

INITIATIVE AND LEADERSHIP

I realize that the place to begin developing the habit of initiative is in the small, commonplace things connected with my daily work; therefore, I will go at my work each day as if I were doing it solely for the purpose of developing this necessary habit of initiative.

I understand that by practicing this habit of taking the initiative in connection with my daily work, I will be not only developing that habit, but I will also be attracting the attention of those who will place greater value on my services as a result of this practice.

Signed..

Regardless of what you are now doing, every day brings you face to face with a chance to render some service, outside of the course of your regular duties, that will be of value to others. In rendering this additional service, of your own accord, you of course understand that you are not doing so with the object of receiving monetary pay. You are rendering this service because it provides you with ways and means of exercising, developing, and making stronger the aggressive spirit of initiative which you must possess before you can ever become an outstanding figure in the affairs of your chosen field of life-work.

Those who work for money alone, and who receive for their pay nothing but money, are always underpaid, no matter how much they receive. Money is necessary, but the big prizes of life cannot be measured in dollars and cents.

No amount of money could possibly take the place of the happiness, joy, and pride that belong to the person who digs a better ditch, builds a better chicken coop, sweeps a cleaner floor, or cooks a better meal. Every normal person loves to create something that is better than the average. The joy of creating a work of art is a joy that cannot be replaced by money or any other form of material possession.

The brand of leadership recommended through this course of instruction is the kind that leads to self-determination, freedom, self-development, enlightenment, and justice. This is the brand that endures. For example, and as a contrast with the brand of leadership through which Napoleon raised himself into prominence, consider our own American commoner, Lincoln. The object of his leadership was to bring truth, justice, and understanding to the people of the United States. Even though he died a martyr to his belief in this brand of leadership, his name has been engraved upon the heart of the world in terms of loving kindness that will never bring aught but good to the world.

10

The Symphony of Success

There are two forms of co-operation to which your attention will be directed in this lesson; namely:

First, the co-operation between people who group themselves together or form alliances for the purpose of attaining a given end, under the principles known as the Law of the Master Mind.

Second, the co-operation between the conscious and the subconscious minds, which forms a reasonable hypothesis of man's ability to contact, communicate with, and draw upon infinite intelligence.

To one who has not given serious thought to this subject, the foregoing hypothesis may seem unreasonable; but follow the evidence of its soundness, and study the facts upon which the hypothesis is based, and then draw your own conclusions.

Let us begin with a brief review of the physical construction of the body:

'We know that the whole body is traversed by a network of nerves which serve as the channels of communication between the indwelling spiritual ego, which we call mind, and the functions of the external organism.

This nervous system is dual. One system, known as the sympathetic, is the channel for all those activities which are not consciously directed by our volition, such as the operation of the digestive organs, the repair of the daily wear and tear of the tissues, and the like.

The other system, known as the voluntary or cerebrospinal system, is the channel through which we receive conscious perception from the physical senses and exercise control over the movements of the body. This system has its center in the brain, while the other has its center in the ganglionic mass at the back of the stomach known as the solar plexus, and sometimes spoken of as the abdominal brain. The cerebro-spinal system is the channel of our volitional or conscious mental action, and the sympathetic system is the channel of that mental action which unconsciously supports the vital functions of the body.

Thus, the cerebro-spinal system is the organ of the conscious mind, and the sympathetic is that of the subconscious mind.

But the interaction of conscious and subconscious minds requires a similar interaction between the corresponding systems of nerves, and one conspicuous connection by which this is provided is the "vagus" nerve. This nerve passes out of the cerebral region as a portion of the voluntary system, and through it, we control the vocal organs; then it passes onward to the thorax, sending out branches to the heart and lungs; and finally, passing through the diaphragm, it loses the outer coating which distinguishes the nerves of the voluntary system and becomes identified with those of the sympathetic system, so forming a connecting link between the two and making the man physically a single entity.

Similarly, different areas of the brain indicate their connection with the objective and subjective activities of the mind respectively. Speaking in a general way, we may assign the frontal portion of the brain to the former and the posterior portion to the latter, while the intermediate portion partakes of the character of both.

The intuitional faculty has its correspondence in the upper area of the brain, situated between the frontal and the posterior portions. Physiologically speaking, it is here that intuitive ideas find entrance. These ideas, at first, are more or less unformed and generalized in character but are nevertheless perceived by the conscious mind; otherwise, we should not be aware of them at all. Then the effort of nature is to bring these ideas into more definite and usable shape. The conscious mind lays hold of them and induces a corresponding vibratory current in the voluntary system of nerves, and this, in turn, induces a similar current in the involuntary system, thus handing the idea over to the subjective mind. The vibratory current, which had first descended from the apex of the brain to the frontal brain and through the voluntary system to the solar plexus, is now reversed and ascends from the solar plexus through the sympathetic system to the posterior brain. This return current indicates the action of the subjective mind.'

If we were to remove the surface portion of the apex of the brain, we should find immediately below it the shining belt of brain substance called the corpus callosum. This is the point of union between the subjective and objective. As the current returns from the solar plexus to this point, it is restored to the objective portion of the brain in a fresh form, which it has acquired by the silent alchemy of the subjective mind. Thus, the conception which was at first only vaguely recognized is restored to the objective mind in a definite and workable form. The objective mind, acting through the frontal brain—the area of comparison and analysis—proceeds to work upon a clearly perceived idea and to bring out the potentialities that are latent in it.

SUBJECTIVE AND OBJECTIVE MIND

The term 'subjective mind' is synonymous with 'subconscious mind,' and 'objective mind' is synonymous with 'conscious mind.' It's important to grasp these distinctions.

By studying this dual system through which the body transmits energy, we discover the precise points where the two systems connect and how we can transmit a thought from the conscious to the subconscious mind.

This cooperative dual nervous system is the most crucial form of cooperation known to humankind, as it allows the principle of evolution to develop precise thought, as described in Lesson Eleven.

When you impress any idea on your subconscious mind through auto-suggestion, you do so with the aid of this dual nervous system. When your subconscious mind formulates a clear plan based on any desire you've impressed upon it, this plan is relayed back to your conscious mind through the same dual nervous system.

This cooperative system of nerves literally forms a direct line of communication between your everyday conscious mind and infinite intelligence.

Understanding how challenging it can be, based on my own initial experiences with this subject, to accept the hypothesis described here, I'll illustrate its validity in a simple way that you can understand and test yourself.

Before going to bed, impress upon your mind the desire to wake up the next morning at a specific time, say 4 A.M. If you couple this impression with a firm determination to wake up at that hour, your subconscious mind will register the impression and awaken you precisely at that time.

Now, you might ask:

'If I can impress my subconscious mind to wake me at a set time, why shouldn't I form the habit of impressing it with other, more important desires?'

We will now discuss cooperation among individuals who unite or form groups to achieve specific objectives. In the second lesson of this course, we referred to this type of cooperation as organized effort.

Cooperation is a recurring theme in almost every lesson of this course. This is inevitable because the course aims to assist students in developing power, and power can only be cultivated through organized effort.

We live in an era dominated by cooperative endeavors. Nearly all successful businesses operate under some form of cooperation. The same holds true in industries, finance, and the professional sectors.

Doctors and lawyers have their alliances for mutual support and protection in the form of Bar Associations and Medical Associations. Bankers have local and national associations for mutual assistance and progress. Retail merchants organize associations for similar purposes.

Automobile owners join clubs and associations. Printers, plumbers, and coal dealers also have their respective associations, all aiming for cooperation.

The objective of all these associations is cooperation. Even laborers have unions, and those who provide working capital and oversee labor efforts form alliances under various names.

Nations too have cooperative alliances, although they may not yet fully comprehend the concept of cooperation. The attempts by the late President Wilson to establish the League of Nations, followed by similar efforts by President Harding under the World Court, illustrate the current trend towards cooperation.

Gradually, humanity is realizing that those who effectively apply the principle of cooperative effort tend to endure longer. This principle applies from the lowest forms of animal life to the highest achievements of human endeavor.

HOW POWER IS DEVELOPED THROUGH CO-OPERATION

As previously discussed, power represents organized effort or energy. Personal power is cultivated by developing, organizing, and aligning the faculties of the mind. This can be achieved by mastering and applying the fifteen fundamental principles upon which this course is built. The detailed process for mastering these principles is thoroughly explained in the sixteenth lesson.

However, developing personal power is only the initial step towards unlocking the potential power available through cooperative or allied efforts, often referred to as group power.

It is widely recognized that individuals who have accumulated substantial fortunes are skilled 'organizers.' This term denotes their ability to engage the cooperative efforts of others who possess talents and skills different from their own.

The primary aim of this course is to elucidate the principles of organized and cooperative (or allied) effort in a manner that allows the student to grasp their significance and integrate them into their personal philosophy.

Consider any business or profession as an example, and upon analysis, it becomes evident that its success hinges on the application of organized and cooperative effort. Take the legal profession, for instance.

If a law firm comprises individuals of only one type of legal mind, it will face significant limitations, even if composed of a dozen competent individuals of that particular type. The complexity of the legal system demands a diversity of talents that no single individual can provide.

Hence, mere organization alone is insufficient to ensure exceptional success; the firm must consist of individuals, each contributing specialized talents that complement those of others within the organization.

A well-organized law firm, for instance, would ideally include specialists in case preparation—individuals with vision and imagination who can harmonize legal principles and case evidence under a comprehensive strategy. However, these individuals may not necessarily possess the skills required for courtroom litigation. Therefore, the firm must also include proficient trial lawyers who excel in court procedures.

Expanding this analysis further reveals that different types of cases require specialists with diverse abilities in both case preparation and trial advocacy. For instance, a lawyer specializing in corporate law may be ill-equipped to handle a criminal case.

In forming a law partnership, a person who understands the principles of organized, cooperative effort would surround himself with specialized talent in every branch of law and legal procedure relevant to his practice. Conversely, someone lacking insight into these principles might choose associates haphazardly, relying more on personal relationships or familiarity rather than considering the specific legal expertise each possesses.

The topic of organized effort has been addressed in previous lessons of this course, but it is revisited here to emphasize the importance of forming alliances or organizations composed of individuals who collectively possess all the necessary talents required to achieve their goals.

In nearly all business endeavors, three essential types of talent are needed: buyers, salespeople, and financial experts. When these three groups organize and coordinate their efforts, they harness a power through cooperation that no single individual within the group could achieve alone.

Many businesses fail because they are disproportionately staffed with only salespeople, financial experts, or buyers. Effective salespeople are often optimistic, enthusiastic, and driven by emotion, while competent financial experts tend to be methodical, cautious, and conservative. Both types of expertise are crucial for business success, but an imbalance without the complementary influence of the other can strain any enterprise.

It is unfortunate for individuals who, due to ignorance or ego, believe they can navigate life independently. Such individuals will inevitably encounter challenges more perilous than mere turbulent waters. All natural laws and the designs of nature are founded on harmonious, cooperative effort, as recognized by those who have achieved great success in the world.

In any conflict, regardless of its nature or cause, the presence of these perilous challenges is evident. Success in life cannot be attained without peaceful, harmonious, cooperative effort. Nor can success be achieved in isolation or independently. Even a hermit living in the wilderness, far removed from civilization, remains dependent on external forces for survival. The more integrated into society one becomes, the more reliant they are on cooperative effort.

Whether a man earns his living through daily labor or from the interest on a fortune he has amassed, he will encounter less resistance and greater success through friendly cooperation with others. Furthermore, those whose philosophy prioritizes cooperation over competition not only attain life's necessities and luxuries with less effort, but also experience a deeper happiness that others may never know.

Fortunes acquired through cooperative effort leave no emotional scars on their owners, a contrast to those amassed through conflict and competitive methods verging on exploitation.

The pursuit of material wealth, whether for basic sustenance or luxury, consumes much of our time in this earthly endeavor. While we may not change this materialistic aspect of human nature, we can alter our approach by embracing cooperation as the foundation of our pursuit.

11

Nurturing Your Greatest Asset

To achieve optimal vigor and harness your body's full potential, it's crucial to grasp two fundamental truths:

1. Your body and mind are inseparable, forming a unified entity—your mindbody.
2. Your mindbody is intimately connected with nature itself.

The health of your mind directly impacts your body, and vice versa. This interconnectedness underscores why you are referred to as a mindbody. Moreover, you are influenced by your surroundings, governed by the same natural laws that regulate trees, mountains, and wildlife.

Maintaining a balanced mindbody hinges on understanding nature's workings and aligning with its forces rather than resisting them.

THE RHYTHMS OF LIFE

Observing the ocean's waves, the cycle of seasons, and the phases of the moon reveals nature's rhythmic patterns. Similarly, your own life progresses through stages—from birth and youth to maturity, old age, and the renewal of generations.

In nature, light, energy, and matter flow in waves, whether expanding outward or bound like particles orbiting an atomic nucleus. Life itself is dynamic, constantly in motion, guided by rhythms—some perceptible, others subtle. This dynamic quality mirrors our affinity for music, which echoes the ebb and flow of our experiences.

Learning to adapt and flow with life's rhythms is essential. Like a sandy beach shaped and enduring through millennia by the ocean's cadence, rigidity and resistance, akin to a breakwater, lead to swift erosion.

Consider your life: Is it rhythmic? Are you alternating work with play, mental exertion with physical activity, eating with fasting, seriousness with humor, and even channeling sexual energy into creative endeavors?

Your subconscious mind works most effectively when your conscious mind is at rest. True inspiration often strikes after your subconscious has been given a task and your conscious mind is engaged in playful activities.

Take Archimedes, for instance, who struggled with a complex problem until he decided to relax in his bath. It was then, as he noticed the water displacement, that his subconscious mind sparked the solution he sought. Bursting from the bath, he exclaimed 'Eureka!' with newfound clarity.

Are you allowing your mind the space to relax through play? Disrupting natural rhythmic patterns can lead to numerous issues. Without a balance of work and relaxation, your body may become overstimulated, potentially resulting in stress-related disorders. Moreover, without highs and lows, the things you cherish may lose their luster. Remember, past failures enhance the sweetness of success.

Continuous happiness would eventually feel mundane—you need the contrast to appreciate joy fully. This principle is central even in marriage counseling, where couples learn that love ebbs and flows like ocean waves. In these troughs, emotions are neutral, but they magnify the peaks of love's intensity. Just as in life, not every wave is of equal magnitude; some are monumental, cherished for their exhilaration and remembered in adversity.

Understanding and living in harmony with the waves and rhythms of your life is essential to aligning yourself with the world.

THE INFLUENCE OF YOUR MIND

Understanding nature as a complex whole, moving with its own rhythms, parallels understanding your mind and body as an integrated unit, each impacting the other.

Humans, uniquely endowed with thought, possess the power to shape their world and comprehend its laws. With belief and conception, ideas can be realized—a testament echoed by countless pioneers who redirected the course of civilization. From millions of years of evolution emerged creatures that walked, swam, and eventually flew. Yet, within two decades of the Wright brothers' unwavering faith in their concept, humanity took to the skies. This power of the mind is not only demonstrated through experience but also affirmed by the wisdom of seers connected to Infinite Intelligence. As Christ proclaimed, 'All things are possible even unto the end of the world.'

Within your mind-body, your mind assumes the higher function. Your body, a marvelously efficient machine, transports your mind and executes its commands. A well-functioning mind is indispensable for a well-functioning body.

Some individuals face physical limitations—difficulty in

movement, vision, or speech. Yet, their powerful minds enable them to lead rich, creative lives. Helen Keller stands as a striking example, alongside Beethoven and Edison, both navigating severe hearing impairments. Franklin Roosevelt, despite struggling to stand, led the nation through its darkest times. Senator Bob Dole, despite a permanently injured arm from World War II, emerged as a formidable political leader.

Throughout history, civilization has been shaped by individuals who, despite physical constraints, possessed minds that operated with fluidity. Fueled by a definite purpose, faith, enthusiasm, and a positive mental attitude, they transcended limitations to achieve remarkable feats. This is the profound influence of the mind.

ESSENTIALS OF SUCCESS AND HAPPINESS

Many principles essential for success also contribute to maintaining a smoothly functioning mind. Having a definite major purpose and a well-executed plan prevents wavering in your efforts. Think of a situation where you were part of a well-coordinated plan—content, at ease, and comfortable with how things unfolded. A well-organized plan brings harmony that satisfies your mind, while anxiety arises from poorly organized ones.

Controlled attention, self-discipline, accurate thinking, personal initiative, learning from setbacks, and going the extra mile are mental tools to structure and execute your plans. They provide satisfaction in achieving each step and overall progress, nourishing a healthy mind.

Possibly the most crucial quality for sound mental health is a positive mental attitude and its components. Fear and its close companion, anxiety, are among the most destructive forces in the human mind. They dampen enthusiasm, erode faith, obscure vision, dull creative efforts, and disrupt harmony and peace of mind—essential elements for maintaining a positive mental attitude and robust mental health.

THE FORCE OF FEAR

Fear and anxiety generate disharmonious, restless agitation in the mind, leading to serious mental imbalances and manifesting physically as severe diseases, potentially leading to death. Increasingly, healing professions recognize that many human ailments stem from mental distress or are significantly worsened by it.

The list of diseases exacerbated by stress is extensive and diverse, including allergies, asthma, skin disorders, hypertension, heart problems, arthritis, colitis, and immune system disorders.

For example, some hay fever sufferers react with sneezing and itching upon seeing goldenrod in a vase. Inform them the plant is artificial, and their symptoms disappear. This simple instance illustrates how the mind can negatively impact the body.

To counter fear, replace it with self-understanding and faith. Let's examine how fear affects your body's mechanisms.

Brief, momentary fear is a natural and necessary response. It prompts quick action to avoid danger, such as stepping away from an oncoming train or avoiding a cliff edge. Once the threat passes, this type of fear dissipates.

Fear also directs bodily functions toward addressing a threat. Consider the ancient scenario of a cave dweller startled by a noise at night. Instantly, the heart rate accelerates, blood flow shifts from digestion to muscles, muscles receive increased blood supply through dilated vessels, while skin vessels contract to minimize blood loss from potential injury. Hearing sharpens, pupils dilate to admit more light, and the adrenal glands release adrenaline, boosting strength for potential combat.

All this physiological preparation is geared towards surviving a battle or pursuit. During the ensuing struggle, adrenaline is expended, and other bodily systems return to their normal states as they step down from heightened readiness. This response has been crucial for our species' survival over millions of years but is not meant to be sustained indefinitely, as it diverts the body from its usual functions. Yet, many of us activate this response daily or even continuously due to living in frequent fear.

To overcome this, you must work on eliminating the causes of your fears:

- Fear of financial loss: Have you established a system to protect and grow your assets?
- Fear of poor health: Have you sought and followed valuable advice?
- Fear of losing love: Have you invested as much effort in nurturing affection as you would in pursuing a significant business opportunity?
- Fear of death: Have you sought guidance and understanding to replace fear with faith?

The list of fears is endless. However, to cultivate a positive mental attitude and develop a mind that functions smoothly and harmoniously with itself and the world, conquering fear and anxiety is essential.

If recurring fears and anxieties persistently hinder your efforts and paralyze you, seek the assistance of a competent counselor. Seeking help demonstrates maturity and commitment to your well-being and your definite major purpose. A short period of therapy can lead to years of happiness.

Always remember: what your mind can conceive and believe, it can achieve. The person who fears slipping on ice often ends up falling. Continually dwelling on fears makes you more vulnerable to those very fears. Therefore, you must overcome fear before it overcomes you.

THE FORCE OF A POSITIVE MENTAL ATTITUDE

The most effective way to banish fear from your mind is to replace it with a Positive Mental Attitude (PMA).

Émile Coué, the French psychologist, provided a simple yet powerful formula for cultivating PMA and maintaining a healthy consciousness: "Every day, in every way, I am getting better and better." Repeat this affirmation multiple times daily until your subconscious mind internalizes and acts upon it, manifesting as improved health.

This technique operates on the principle of autosuggestion—relying on your belief in the statement. To strengthen this belief, integrate the affirmation into your mental environment. Recognize that your mind is profoundly influenced by its surroundings, and by saturating your environment with positive thoughts, you will gradually adopt and embody them.

EATING HABITS

The primary purpose of food is to provide the body with essential nutrients for maintaining optimal function and repair. Your dietary choices should align with this fundamental objective alone.

Consider your digestive system as a complex factory. For it to operate efficiently, it requires a balanced supply of various nutrients in appropriate quantities. Providing an improper mix of nutrients results in incomplete tasks, makeshift solutions, and accumulation of excess materials within the factory. Eventually, this imbalance leads to structural damage—walls bulge, roofs collapse—and the factory either ceases operations or requires extensive and costly repairs.

Nutritional Guidelines for Balanced Eating

Nutritional science continually evolves as researchers deepen their understanding of the human body. While staying informed about new findings is crucial, avoiding dietary fads is equally important. Here are some fundamental principles to maintain a balanced diet:

1. **Emphasize Fresh Fruits and Vegetables**: These should form the largest part of your meals. They provide a complex mix of vitamins, minerals, and trace elements that your body easily absorbs.
2. **Include Complex Carbohydrates**: Foods like whole grains, breads, and potatoes should constitute a significant portion of your diet. They provide sustained energy and essential nutrients.
3. **Moderate Protein Intake**: Lean meats, fish, and dairy products are important sources of protein. However, avoid making protein the main focus of every meal. Enjoy small portions of these foods.
4. **Limit Fats and Sugars**: Reduce your intake of butter, oils, and deep-fried foods. Minimize consumption of sugars found in candies, colas, and other sugary treats, as they offer little nutritional value beyond calories.
5. **Ensure Variety:** Your body requires a broad spectrum of nutrients, so vary your food choices. Avoid dismissing certain foods with the excuse of preference rather than

necessity. Mental gymnastics that rationalize a limited diet may hinder your health and success.

Avoid Emotional Eating: Refrain from eating when feeling angry, frightened, or worried. In such states, your body is not primed to digest food efficiently. Furthermore, habitual eating in response to stress can lead to weight gain and health issues.

Moderation in Lifestyle and Relaxation Techniques

Maintaining moderation in both food and alcohol consumption is crucial for overall well-being. Excesses in either can overwhelm your body and become ways to avoid confronting underlying issues. If moderation becomes challenging, seeking support from professionals or organizations like Alcoholics Anonymous or Overeaters Anonymous can provide valuable assistance.

Rhythms in Relaxation

Achieving true relaxation involves consciously setting aside worries and distractions from the day. Simply collapsing into a chair and declaring relaxation isn't effective because your mind will naturally fixate on lingering concerns. Instead, choose a specific activity to engage in, such as kite flying, gardening, reading, or any absorbing hobby that captivates your attention.

Avoid relying on passive activities like television or frequenting bars for relaxation. Cultivating diverse interests and practicing controlled meditation can significantly enhance mental clarity and resilience. Engaging in physical activities not only relaxes the mind but also strengthens the body.

Throughout the day, incorporate short breaks for relaxation to alleviate tension and allow your subconscious mind to process information. Activities like reading a magazine, listening to language tapes, or solving puzzles contribute to mental rejuvenation rather than wasting time.

Sleep

Quality sleep is essential for physical and mental rejuvenation. Attempting to boost productivity by reducing sleep is counterproductive. Aim for six to eight hours of sleep each night to support optimal body function and mental clarity. Even during sleep, your subconscious continues to work, processing and consolidating information.

Insomnia often stems from an inability to unwind before bed. Avoid intense physical activity right before sleep and instead, wind down with calming activities. Engage in light conversation with your partner, perform relaxing routines like brushing your teeth or gentle stretching, or establish bedtime rituals that signal your body it's time to sleep.

Exercise

Incorporating exercise into your routine ideally accompanies relaxation and play. While relaxation and play benefit your mind, exercise primarily enhances your physical well-being but also offers significant mental advantages.

To maintain strong heart and lung function, engage in aerobic exercise for at least twenty minutes, three times a week. The intensity of your exercise should be tailored to your age and physical condition. Trainers at local gyms or YMCA centers can guide you in designing a simple and affordable exercise regimen. Before starting any exercise program, consult your doctor for personalized advice.

Exercise serves as a powerful stimulant for both mental and physical vigor, dispelling lethargy while cultivating persistence and concentration. Insights from athletic training, which delve into human potential, offer valuable techniques applicable to your pursuit of success. For instance, Bill Bowerman's experience as a track coach inspired innovations that propelled Nike to become America's leading shoe manufacturer.

Sex and Sublimation

Sex is a fundamental and constructive drive, albeit susceptible to misuse. It underpins the creative forces that advance human progress, contributing to the construction of cathedrals, universities, and nations. The desire for sex motivates us to strive for the well-being of others, fostering kindness and empathy.

Recognize sex as a natural desire without fear or denial. However, like all desires, it must be directed towards specific goals rather than becoming an end in itself. Pursuing sex alone undermines faith in oneself, a definite purpose, and moral standards.

Achieving intimacy requires constructive effort in building committed relationships. By channeling sexual desires into nurturing and sustaining relationships, not only do you fulfill personal desires but also achieve significant accomplishments.

To optimize personal growth, balance sex with sublimation in a rhythmic pattern, similar to balancing work and play.

Effective Mind-Body Stimulants

Boosting your mind-body connection is crucial for maintaining peak performance. Many effective stimulants are already part of your daily life; you just need to be mindful of their impact and actively seek them out:

- **Sexual expression or sublimated sexual drive**: Energizes the mind, enhancing rapid and inspired thinking.
- **Love**: The ultimate aim of sexual desire, it serves a similar purpose and combined with sexual expression, it becomes a powerful motivator.
- **Focusing on your burning obsession**: A strong stimulant that drives intense focus and creativity.
- **Work**: Engage in small, satisfying tasks like making a phone call or writing a thank-you note to express creativity and satisfaction.
- **Exercise**: Releases pent-up energy, relieves frustration, and boosts brain function with increased blood flow and oxygen.
- **Play**: Allows the subconscious to work freely and creatively.
- **Music**: Utilize rhythms and beats to either boost enthusiasm or calm down as needed.
- **Friendship**: Discussing problems and sharing laughter with friends serves as a great mental stimulant.
- **Children**: Building strong relationships with your children and spending quality time with them can inspire and renew self-confidence and faith.
- **Mastermind alliances**: Tap into the enthusiasm and experience of others to boost your own motivation and problem-solving abilities.
- **Autosuggestion**: Implant positive ideas in your mind to reinforce motivation and confidence whenever needed.
- **Faith and religion**: Draw on their assurances to renew your sense of purpose and motivation.

Remember, your mental and physical health are intertwined. Strengthening one positively affects the other. Your mind directs your actions like a navigator guiding a ship to success. Therefore, prioritize preserving, protecting, and nurturing both your mind and body to achieve the success you desire.

12

Footprints in the Sands of Time

What Makes a Personality Attractive? An attractive personality is not just a matter of appearance but encompasses various aspects that draw others towards you. Here are the key elements that contribute to an attractive personality —merge to form a single paragraph—increase font size of "W"— consistency with other chapters

1. **Character**: The foundation of your personality lies in your character. It's the essence of who you are, shaped by your thoughts, values, and actions. Integrity, kindness, and authenticity are traits that often attract others.
2. **Appearance**: While superficial, your outward appearance plays a significant role in forming first impressions. The style and appropriateness of your clothing, along with grooming, can enhance your overall appeal.
3. **Mannerisms and Gestures**: Simple actions like the way you shake hands or maintain eye contact can communicate

confidence, respect, and warmth, making a positive impression on others.

4. **Eyes and Expression**: The eyes are said to be windows to the soul. A genuine, expressive gaze can convey sincerity, empathy, and depth, allowing others to connect with you on a deeper level.
5. **Vitality and Presence**: Personal magnetism, often referred to as charisma, stems from the vitality and energy you exude. It's a combination of enthusiasm, passion, and the ability to engage and inspire others.
6. **Communication Skills**: How you articulate your thoughts, listen attentively, and express empathy influences how others perceive you. Effective communication fosters understanding and connection.
7. **Positive Attitude**: Optimism and a positive outlook on life can be infectious. They attract others who are drawn to your resilience, enthusiasm for challenges, and ability to find solutions.
8. **Emotional Intelligence**: Being aware of your emotions and understanding those of others allows for empathetic responses and effective interpersonal relationships.
9. **Authenticity**: Being true to yourself and genuine in your interactions builds trust and credibility. Authenticity resonates with others, fostering meaningful connections.
10. **Continuous Improvement**: Cultivating these traits and continuously working on personal growth and development enhances your attractiveness over time.

Ultimately, an attractive personality goes beyond surface-level impressions. It's a combination of inner qualities and outward expressions that create a compelling presence, making you someone others are naturally drawn to.

HOW TO ATTAIN A PLEASING PERSONALITY

Let's explore the methods to develop a pleasing personality, starting with the foundational element: character.

Character

A pleasing personality hinges fundamentally on a strong, positive character. Through the principle of telepathy, you unconsciously communicate the essence of your character to others, often evoking an intuitive sense of trustworthiness or skepticism in them upon first meeting.

You can adorn yourself in the latest fashion and behave impeccably, but if your heart harbors traits like greed, envy, hatred, jealousy, avarice, or selfishness, you'll only attract those whose inner qualities mirror your own. Like attracts like, ensuring that those drawn to you reflect your own internal nature.

Even if you wear a manufactured smile or master the art of handshaking to perfection, without genuine earnestness of purpose, these outward signs of a pleasing personality lack the essential vitality to attract others—they may even repel.

So, how does one cultivate character?

The first step in character development is strict self-discipline.

Steps to Develop a Pleasing Personality

First: Identify individuals whose characters embody the qualities you aspire to cultivate within yourself. Using the method described in Lesson Two, employ autosuggestion to appropriate these desired qualities. Visualize a council table in your imagination where these individuals gather each night.

Write clear statements outlining the specific traits you wish to acquire from each person. Audibly affirm to yourself that you are developing these qualities. As you do so, visualize the figures seated around your imaginary table, as detailed in Lesson Two.

Second: Employ the principles outlined in Lesson One to practice self-control over your thoughts. Keep your mind vibrant with positive thoughts. Let your dominant thought be a clear image of the person you are intentionally shaping through this process. At least twelve times a day, when you have a moment alone, close your eyes and focus your thoughts on the figures gathered at your imaginary council table. Have unwavering faith that you are progressively embodying the character traits of these figures.

Third: Daily, seek out at least one person (and more if possible) who possesses admirable qualities deserving of praise, and genuinely praise them. Ensure your praise is sincere and earnest, not mere flattery. Speak with conviction that impresses those you commend. Observe the impact: your sincere praise will greatly benefit the recipients and cultivate in you a habit of recognizing and appreciating the strengths of others. The profound effects of openly and enthusiastically praising others will enhance your self-respect and elicit gratitude from those around you. Through the law of attraction, those you praise will begin to see in you the qualities you admire in them. Your success in applying this formula will directly correlate with your belief in its efficacy.

I not only believe this approach is sound—I know it is. I've successfully applied it myself and taught others to do the same. Therefore, I confidently assure you that you can achieve equal success using it.

Moreover, with the help of this formula, you can develop a compelling personality so rapidly that you'll astonish those around you. The development of such a personality is entirely within your control, which gives you a significant advantage. At the same time, it places upon you the responsibility for any failure or neglect to exercise this privilege.

No one can aspire to leadership in any significant endeavor without acquiring the ability to speak persuasively and with conviction. Even if a salesperson never gives a public speech, developing this skill enhances their ability to communicate persuasively in everyday conversations.

Let's summarize the key factors essential to developing an attractive personality:

1. Cultivate a habit of taking genuine interest in others, and actively seek out and praise their good qualities.
2. Develop the ability to speak forcefully and convincingly, both in casual conversation and in public speaking situations where greater volume is required.
3. Dress in a manner that suits your physique and aligns with your professional role.
4. Build a positive character using the formula outlined in this lesson.
5. Master the art of handshaking to convey warmth and enthusiasm.
6. Draw others to you by first showing genuine interest in them.
7. Remember, your only limitations, within reason, are those you set in your own mind.

These seven points encompass the essential factors for developing an attractive personality, but it's important to emphasize that such a personality doesn't develop on its own. It emerges when you commit to the disciplined approach described here, with a steadfast determination to become the person you aspire to be.

Put aside any grievances and refrain from provoking unnecessary arguments. Replace any tinted lenses through which you perceive life negatively with the bright sunlight of friendliness. Discard the urge to criticize and knock down; remember, life's greatest rewards await those who build, not destroy. The person who constructs a house is an artist; the one who dismantles it is a scavenger. If you carry grievances, the world might heed your bitter complaints if caught unawares, but if you radiate friendliness and optimism, people will listen because they genuinely want to.